CONTENTS

A Sense of English

Conditionals and Modal Verbs

Charlie de Wirtz

FIRST EDITION

PUBLISHED BY LUXAN PUBLISHERS

First Published in 2007

Luxan Publishers
12, Naomi Close
Eastbourne
East Sussex
BN20 7UU
England

© Charlie de Wirtz

ISBN: 978-0-9546088-4-2
CD ISBN: 978-0-9546088-5-9

A catalogue record for this book is available from the British Library.

GUIDE TO THE USE OF THE CD

- Each Module contains either 40 or 50 numbered sentences, all of which are examples of that Module's particular subject (e.g. The First Conditional, The Second Conditional etc).

- At the end of each Module (but before the summary) you will be instructed to listen to those example sentences on numbered tracks on the CD.

- The summary at the end of each Module provides further example sentences of the subject studied.

- After reading each summary there is another track to listen to. The tracks that follow the summary contain a series of conversations that provide a context for the sentences given in the summary. There are transcripts of these tracks at the back of the book – tracks 2, 4, 6, 8, 11, 14, 17 and 20.

- The CD tracks contain a mixture of American and British English.

Please note that in the transcripts and throughout "A Sense of English" the spelling has been standardized to **British English** to avoid unnecessary confusion.

INTRODUCTION TO PART ONE

Modules 1-4 deal with the **Conditional** sentences in English. They are sentences that have two parts - a condition (usually using the word 'if') and a result.

There are three classic structures which students generally learn:

First Conditional

If + Present Simple + Future (will do / going to do)

Second Conditional

If + Past Simple + Conditional (would do)

Third Conditional

If + Past Perfect + Conditional Perfect (would have done)

The **First Conditional** is used to talk about real possibilities.

In this way it is different from the **Second** and **Third Conditionals**. They express conditions belonging to the imaginary world.

The above structures are the most common types of sentence, but there are many ways in which **Conditional** sentences deviate from these classic structures.

The first three Modules of this book will deal with each of the three **Conditional** types in turn. The fourth Module deals some variant types of **Conditional** sentence.

Firstly, you will see how the classic structure works. Then you will learn different ways in which the classic structure can change (this is very often related to the use of modal verbs), and how these changes alter the meaning and feeling of the sentence.

The change in meaning is often very subtle. Understanding these subtleties and being able to use them correctly in your own spoken and written English is the overriding purpose of this book.

It's about developing "A Sense of English".

THE FIRST CONDITIONAL

The important point to understand about the **First Conditional** is that it is used to talk about real possibilities within the real world.

As you have seen in the introduction to this section, the **First Conditional** has what can be called a 'classic structure', which is:

If + Present Simple + Future (will do / going to do)

About 70% of **First Conditional** sentences are formed using this tense structure. That leaves an important 30% or so that are formed differently.

Of this 30%, it is nearly always the second part of the sentence that changes. Instead of using **will** or **going to**, a modal verb might be used, like **might**, **can** or **could**. There is then a change in the sense of the sentence.

Understanding these kinds of nuances – and being able to put them into effect in your personal communication - is what gaining "a sense of English" is all about.

You will see and hear plenty of examples shortly. But let's start by looking at ten classic structure sentences.

CLASSIC STRUCTURE:
If + Present Simple + Future (will / going to)

The first step is simply to read sentences 1-10, understand them, and think about their context. Try to imagine who might be speaking to whom and why.

1 **If you clean the bathroom, I'll wash the car.**

2 **If he comes home before 10.00, I'll get him to call you.**

3 We're going to take a holiday if the house sells. *

4 Mum'll be so happy if you come at Christmas. *

5 If Manchester United beat Real Madrid, the manager will become a legend.

6 If you practise every day, you'll improve quickly.

7 If I have time, I'll do it tonight.

8 If you don't put that money in the bank, you'll spend it.

9 You'll be surprised at the cost of living if you go to Prague. *

10 If you pass your exams, we're going to take you skiing for a week in Switzerland.

*Notice how the two parts of the sentence have been switched round. Grammatically, this is possible in all **Conditional** sentences.*

When thinking about the context, you have to think about who might be speaking, to whom, and what the likely situation is. Sometimes the situation is obvious, other times the sentence could fit into a variety of contexts.

To make my suggestions more readable, I have given names to the characters involved in each situation.

Even though it might seem easy, take a moment to read them and compare them with the ideas you had. Remember that my ideas are only suggestions – there is very rarely only one correct answer.

1 If you clean the bathroom, I'll wash the car.

John makes a suggestion to his wife Angela about how to divide household chores.

2 **If he comes home before 10.00, I'll get him to call you.**

Andrew has called his brother Mike, but he is not at home, and Susan (Mike's wife) speaks to her brother-in-law.

3 **We're going to take a holiday if the house sells.**

David and Sarah have decided that if they manage to sell their house they will use some of the money for a nice holiday.

4 **Mum'll be so happy if you come at Christmas.**

Chris tries to persuade his sister to come and spend Christmas at home.

5 **If Manchester United beat Real Madrid, the manager will become a legend.**

A pundit's assessment before a big football match.

6 **If you practise every day, you'll improve quickly.**

A sports coach gives encouragement.

7 **If I have time, I'll do it tonight.**

Mark promises his mum to try and clean his room tonight.

8 **If you don't put that money in the bank, you'll spend it.**

A father warns his son.

9 **You'll be surprised at the cost of living if you go to Prague.**

James informs his friend that Prague is not as cheap (or expensive) as he imagines.

10 **If you pass your exams, we're going to take you skiing for a week in Switzerland.**

A father gives an incentive to his son to study hard.

Sometimes it is not clear just from the written words what the speaker's feeling is. Hearing the sentences spoken, and the intonation used, would give a strong indication of the speaker's intention and the mood his/her words are creating.

You will be able to hear the numbered sentences in this Module on the CD later on.

IMPORTANT

1.   Can you see how all the sentences are talking about real possibilities?

Sentence 1 is a suggestion of a real course of action. Sentence 2 means Mike will wait until 10.00, knowing there is a real possibility his brother will call him. In sentence 3 a real plan has been made, and so on.

All the sentences are talking about real possibilities that depend on real events - in the real world.

2.   Usually the First Conditional talks about a possible action or situation and its consequence.

Look again at the ten sentences and see how that is true.

3.   Very often in spoken English a contraction takes place between the subject and the word will (i.e. I'll, you'll, etc.)

There are no rules about when a contraction should or should not take place. Usually students of English struggle with contractions and just stick to the easier separation of words – "I will go..." – when they speak. However, if you want to sound natural when speaking English, you should develop a feel for the way that native speakers use contractions.

SEE APPENDIX ONE

▼   Have a look at sentences 11-20 (some of which will deviate from the classic structure) which give further examples of advice and warnings/threats:

If you're afraid of spiders, don't watch that movie!

12 If he wants to be a good teacher of children, he must learn to be more patient.

13 If you're late again, you won't be on the team.

14 You should make an appointment to see the doctor if you don't feel better by tomorrow.

15 I think he'll be unhappy if he marries her. *

16 I might give in my notice if I don't get a pay rise.

17 If the party continues after midnight, you must keep the noise down or the neighbours will complain.

18 If she wants to write the book, I think she'll have to give up her job. *

19 If her parents invite you on the trip to South Africa, you should definitely go!

20 If the government doesn't pay the ransom by Friday, the kidnappers are going to kill the hostages.

*Notice how the result is prefaced by "I think". This is perfectly possible in **Conditional** sentences, with the effect of emphasizing a personal opinion over a fairly certain consequence.*

SEE APPENDIX TWO

Let's talk about the imperative first. It is used in **First Conditional** sentences to make requests:

21 If you go to Pisa while you're in Italy, send me a postcard of the Leaning Tower!

This sentence is informal. The use of the imperative often (but not always) implies informality – a friend talking to a friend, or a family member to another family member.

7

The request can be made more polite in two ways:

22 **If you see John at the party, please say hello from me.**

23 **If you go to the supermarket, could you buy me some shampoo?**

In sentence 22, using "please" before the imperative is a simple and clear way to make a request more formal or polite.

Making the second part of the sentence into a question, as in sentence 23, means that you are no longer using the imperative. It is an even more polite way of making a request, and it involves the use of a modal verb.

Now we need to think about how using a modal verb – as a replacement for **will** or **going to** - alters the sense of a sentence.

Three pairs of sentences now follow that compare using **will/ going to** with other modal verbs. Explanations of the nuances in meaning follow, but before reading them, think for yourself about how the particular modal verb used affects the meaning.

In the summary at the end of this Module, you will see many further example sentences to help deepen your understanding.

What is the difference between these two sentences?

24 **If the weather's good tomorrow, we're going for a picnic.**

25 **If the weather's good tomorrow, we could go for a picnic.**

This one should be fairly easy. Sentence 24 describes something already decided, a plan that has already been made.

Sentence 25, however, is a suggestion that is being made. It is a sentence that requires a response from the listener – e.g. "Yes, let's do that – it's a good idea."

Could expresses a possibility, and can therefore be used as a way of making a suggestion. Sentence 25, then, has the same effect as a question, because it demands a response.

▼ How about these two?

26 **If I finish what I have to do, I might go out for a drink.**

27 **If I finish what I have to do, I will go out for a drink.**

These two are slightly more difficult. The key question to consider is: What will decide whether the speaker goes out for a drink or not?

SEE APPENDIX THREE

▼ What about these two?

28 **If the company places an order of over five thousand books, we'll offer them free carriage.**

29 **If the company places an order of over five thousand books, we must offer them free carriage.**

Will always expresses certainty. So sentence 28 is a declaration of intention.

Sentence 29 is an expression of obligation that the selling company feels. It's a strong compulsion that they put on themselves to make some favourable terms for the company doing business with them.

The difference between these two sentences is in the feeling more than the meaning. Both express the same result — free carriage is almost certainly going to be offered — but one focuses on pure intention while the other emphasizes the strong feeling of obligation.

THE FIRST CONDITIONAL

Now it's your turn to write some suitable **First Conditional** sentences for the following situations.

Of course, there are no fixed answers here. I have given some suggested answers with some added explanatory notes where appropriate.

It is important that you check your answers with a native speaker to see if what you come up with is suitable or not.

1. You want to go out for a drink with your friend, but have to wait until your girlfriend calls you from abroad. (Sentence 30)

2. Mike is taking an important exam next month and has to study a lot in order to pass. (Sentence 31)

3. You want to go to Italy in September but it depends on your financial situation. (Sentence 32)

4. A boss tells his secretary to inform Mr. Smith (if he calls) that he is unavailable. (Sentence 33)

5. Your younger sister wants to go out tonight but you tell her that she must finish her homework first. (Sentence 34)

6. You have decided not to buy roses for your wife if they cost over £10. (Sentence 35)

7. You suggest an exchange with your Korean friend to teach each other your language. (Sentence 36)

8. Promise your friend something you will do for them if they visit your country. (Sentence 37)

9. The weather forecast for tomorrow is light showers. You had planned to go the beach – suggest an alternative plan. (Sentence 38)

10. Your friend (who is 45) wants to quit his job – advise him against the idea. (Sentence 39)

11. You have to go to London tomorrow but feel tired right now. You are considering driving, but it will depend on how you feel tomorrow. (Sentence 40)

SUGGESTED ANSWERS

30 **If my girlfriend calls me before 9.00, I'll join you for a drink.**

> For the sense of the context, it's important to put some specification of time here. Whether you go out for a drink or not doesn't depend on *whether* your girlfriend calls, it depends on *when* she calls. If she calls after midnight, for example, it will be too late to go.

31 **If Mike studies a lot, he'll pass the exam.**

> It would be fine to use **should** here instead of **will**. The difference is that **should** suggests "probably he'll pass". **Will** suggests a greater degree of certainty.

32 **If I have enough money in September, I'll go to Italy.**

33 **If Mr Smith calls, tell him I'm unavailable.**

34 **You can go out if you finish your homework.**

> **Can** is used here as a way of giving permission to do something.

35 **I won't buy roses if they cost more than £10.**

> **Not going to** would also be fine to use here. The difference is simply in the timing of the decision – **going to** suggests that you have previously thought about something and come to a decision. **Will** is often a decision that has been made very recently or right at that moment.

36 **I'll teach you English if you teach me Korean.**

> You could equally use **could** here.

37 **If you come to Japan, I'll take you to a sushi bar.**

38 **If it rains tomorrow, we could go to the cinema.**

A suggestion that requires a response.

39 **If you give up your job now, it'll be difficult to find another one.**

40 **If I'm not too tired in the morning, I might drive.**

Remember, you could use **will** here, but it would mean that the speaker has already decided. This sentence, as it stands, means that even if I'm not tired tomorrow, I might not drive. This is very important. **Will** implies certainty, the decision has been made. **Might** implies that the person has not decided yet. So, his/her decision doesn't only depend on whether he is tired or not. There are other factors which will influence his decision tomorrow.

TRACK ONE

Now listen to Track One on the CD.

THE FIRST CONDITIONAL

SUMMARY

In the summary, my aim is to give you more example sentences to further develop your sense of the **First Conditional**.

We have seen how the **First Conditional** has the following classic or common structure:

If + Present Simple + will do / going to do

If I get away from the office on time, I'll pick you up from the airport.

We have seen how it can also take the following two forms:

If + Present Simple + Imperative

If we're not back by 5.00, put the chicken in the oven.

If + Present Simple + Modal Verb

If Bill drinks coffee after 9.00, he can't sleep.
If you go to Argentina, you must try the popular soup called "Guisos".

Here is a breakdown of the major uses of the **First Conditional**:

SUGGESTION

If you take next week off, we could have a few days away together.

Your parents could buy a villa in Florida if they sell the flat in Manhattan.

DEAL / PROMISE / PERMISSION

If you fix my car for free, I'll give your son ten hours free maths tuition.

If my son passes his driving test, I'm going to buy him a car.

You guys can play on the computer until supper if you promise to wash up.

REQUEST

If you call Uncle Sam tonight, thank him again for the birthday present.

Could you tell Sarah to call me if you see her?

ASSESSMENT

If urban migration continues to increase at the current rate, there'll be an even bigger poverty problem in a few years.

You should pass the exam if you study hard.

ADVICE / THREATEN

If you refuse to call the doctor, you should at least take some aspirin.

If you come to my house asking for money again, I'll call the police.

Whatever the use of the **First Conditional**, it always speaks about some action and a result in the real world.

TRACK TWO

Now listen to Track Two on the CD.

THE SECOND CONDITIONAL

As opposed to the **First Conditional**, the **Second Conditional** talks about the imaginary world. It imagines either a situation that is not real now (but could be later) or a situation that is impossible and can never become real.

The classic structure of the **Second Conditional** is the following:

If + Past Simple + Conditional (would do)

Just as with the **First Conditional**, sometimes **would** is replaced by another modal verb (**could**, **might** etc.)

Although the tense used in the first part of the sentence is the past simple, the meaning is not past. That is the first thing to be clear about with the **Second Conditional**. The main meaning of the **Second Conditional** is to imagine something that is not true or real at the moment. It never talks about a past action or event.

As we did with the **First Conditional**, let's look at ten **Second Conditional** sentences that use the classic structure.

Just as you did before, think about the meaning of the sentences. Once you understand the concept of the **Second Conditional** it is very easy to use.

1 **If I had time, I'd read the newspaper every day.**

2 **John and Lisa would get married tomorrow if their parents agreed.**

3 **I'd move to South America if I didn't have a family.**

4 **If that house were on the market, we'd make an offer for it.**

5 We'd travel the world if we had enough money.

6 If he was ill, he wouldn't be able to play football.

7 Don't speak to me like that! If your father was here, he'd be furious.

8 If I didn't have to work tomorrow morning, I'd take you to the airport

9 Don't tell John about it – if he knew the truth, he'd be devastated.

10 If he studied more, he'd pass the exam.

SEE APPENDIX FOUR

The **Second Conditional** imagines something that is not real at the moment (and may never be real).

Have a look now at my explanations of what the ten sentences mean:

1 If I had time, I'd read the newspaper every day.

Reality: I don't have time to read the newspaper every day.

2 John and Lisa would get married tomorrow if their parents agreed.

Reality: Their parents don't agree to their idea of getting married.

3 I'd move to South America if I didn't have a family.

Reality: I have a family, so I can't move to South America.

4 If that house were on the market, we'd make an offer for it.

Reality: That house we are interested in is not on the market.

5 We'd travel the world if we had enough money.

Reality: We don't have enough money to travel the world.

6 **If he was ill, he wouldn't be able to play football.**

Reality: He is not really ill, but he is playing football.
(The context of this sentence is almost certainly that "he" is pretending to be ill, and the speaker is concluding that he can't be ill if he is able to play football.)

7 **Don't speak to me like that! If your father was here, he'd be furious.**

Reality: The father is not present to tell off his son/daughter for being rude.

8 **If I didn't have to work tomorrow morning, I'd take you to the airport.**

Reality: I have to work, so I can't take you to the airport.

9 **Don't tell John about it – if he knew the truth, he'd be devastated.**

Reality: John doesn't know the truth, and it's better to protect him from it.

10 **If he studied more, he'd pass the exam.**

Reality: He is not studying enough at the moment.

 IMPORTANT

1.   Can you see how every time the sentences imagine the opposite of the real situation?

Often the sense is dreamlike – the speakers are expressing a kind of "Ah, I wish..." Look at sentences 1-5. The feeling behind each one is a wish.

2.   Notice again how the contraction is used so often (I'd, we'd, etc.).

Let me stress again the importance of your developing a feel for contractions in your spoken English.

SEE APPENDIX FIVE

THE SECOND CONDITIONAL

▼ The **Second Conditional** is also used to give advice. Have a look at the special structure that is used to do this in sentences 11-15:

11 **If I were you I'd break up with him.**

12 **If I were you, I'd take some private lessons.**

13 **If I were him, I'd go to the doctor with that cough.**

14 **I wouldn't give John any money if I were his parents.**

15 **I'd look for another job if I were you.**

IMPORTANT

1. The speakers are imagining what they would do if they were in the position of the person they are advising. "If I were you...", in other words, "If I was in your (or whoever's) situation...".

2. As was discussed in Appendix Four, note that the grammatically correct structure is "If I *were* you...", not "If I *was* you...".

These sentences should be easy enough to understand.

▼ The **Second Conditional** sometimes talks about imaginary situations which are also impossible. Something is imagined that can never be true.

Have a look at sentences 16-20 which give examples of this use:

16 **If there were dinosaurs on the earth now, life would be very interesting.**

17 **If I were American, I wouldn't vote for the Democrats.**

18

18 If you were the national team coach, you'd change the system completely, wouldn't you?

19 If I had my university days to do over again, I'd spend more time studying.

20 John would take up golf if he could walk without a stick.

Each sentence is talking about something impossible. So the **Second Conditional** is again being used to express something imaginary, but what is being expressed in each of these sentences is something that can never be true. (Sentence 18 is debatable – we assume two ordinary fans are talking who have no aspirations about applying for the coach's job!)

As you know, sometimes **Second Conditional** sentences follow a different structure. The modal verbs **could** and **might** can often replace the use of **would** in the second part of the sentence.

On rare occasions, other modal verbs can be used as well, but here we are going to focus on **might** and **could** as they are the ones that are almost always used.

Sentences 21-28 give some examples of this.

The best way of understanding how using **could** and **might** alter the sense of the sentence is to compare them with the use of **would**.

Have a look at the following pairs of sentences that highlight these differences:

21 If I went to Brazil, I could visit my friend.

22 If I went to Brazil, I'd visit my friend.

SEE APPENDIX SIX

23 I could write the essay tonight if I had my notes.

24 I'd write the essay tonight if I had my notes.

The difference here should now be clearer to you.

Sentence 23 expresses what would be *possible* if I had my notes. Sentence 24 expressed my will and *intention* if I had my notes.

These sentences don't carry an opposite meaning. The speaker in sentence 23 would probably do his/her essay if they had their notes just like the speaker in 24. It is simply that by using **could** the possibility is being emphasized as opposed to the intention.

25 If you listened to the teacher you'd learn something.

26 If you listened to the teacher you might learn something!

Sentence 25 again expresses a certainty, i.e. the only reason you don't learn anything is that you don't listen to the teacher.

In sentence 26, **might** is used. **Might** expresses possibility, like **could**. Notice how an exclamation mark is used here – it fits the sense of the sentence. Why?

The sense is that the student who doesn't listen to the teacher probably doesn't believe that he/she can learn. They don't have confidence in their own ability. The speaker is trying to persuade them to give themselves and the teacher a chance - "Don't give up, start listening and making an effort, and you might be pleasantly surprised.".

27 If you tried Chinese food you might like it!

28 If you tried Chinese food I think you'd like it.

SEE APPENDIX SEVEN

▼ With some of the sentences you have read in this Module, it might be difficult for you to see what is the difference between a **First Conditional** sentence and a **Second Conditional** sentence.

Sometimes it can be difficult to understand which one you should use.

Look back at sentences 21 and 22 from this Module and change them into **First Conditional** sentences.

SEE APPENDIX EIGHT

▼ Have a look at two more **Second Conditional** sentences, with the **First Conditional** equivalents written underneath in brackets:

29 **If they played football every week, their wives would complain.**

(If they play football every week, their wives will complain.)

30 **If you moved back home again, the kids would be so happy.**

(If you move back home again, the kids'll be so happy.)

In sentence 29, the **Second Conditional** sentence means that the husbands don't play football every week, and there is nothing to suggest that is going to change. The sentence only imagines what the result would be if the situation was different.

The **First Conditional** sentence is talking about the real world, and a real possibility of the husbands deciding to play every week. It suggests that a decision has to be made – perhaps they have to tell the manager soon how often they will be available to play.

The difference between the **First** and **Second Conditional** in sentence 29 should be clear.

SEE APPENDIX NINE

THE SECOND CONDITIONAL

Now it's your turn to write some suitable **Second Conditional** sentences for the following situations. This exercise is just like the one in Module One.
I have given some possible answers underneath and some explanatory notes where appropriate.

Let me stress again that it is important you check your answers with a native speaker.

1. You'd like to travel the world, but need to win the lottery first. (Sentence 31)

2. Your friend works long hours behind a desk and is worried because he is becoming fat and needs to lose weight. Give him some advice. (Sentence 32)

3. Mike would like to play tennis every day after work, but he always has to work overtime. (Sentence 33)

4. You and your husband/wife dream about what having a bigger garden would mean to your two young children. (Sentence 34)

5. Your mother thinks that the reason Mark and Laura (your children, her grandchildren) are always tired is because they don't sleep enough. (Sentence 35)

6. You have just witnessed a crime and are considering going to the police, but you are undecided as it occurs to you that if you do go, there is a possibility you will have to go to court. (Sentence 36)

7. Your friend has never learnt to drive because they are afraid, but you try to make them think about an advantage of being able to drive. (Sentence 37)

8. You'd like to live in China, but because of visa restrictions, in order to do so you need to marry a Chinese person. (Sentence 38)

9. Your friend's parents want to sell their house quickly, but the housing market is in a slump, so you advice your friend that they should wait. (Sentence 39)

10. Imagine the very interesting (but highly unlikely) situation of you becoming President/Prime Minister of your country. Mention something you would do. (Sentence 40)

THE SECOND CONDITIONAL

SUGGESTED ANSWERS

31 **If I won the lottery, I'd travel the world.**

> A clear declaration of a dream and an intention of what you **would** do if the dream came true. **Would** means you have already decided.

32 **I'd join a gym and do some exercise if I were you.**

> A classic sentence of advice using the structure you know.

33 **If Mike didn't have to work overtime, he'd play tennis every evening after work.**

> Use **would** because Mike is clear about what he'd like to do if it were possible.

34 **If we had a bigger garden, the children could play in it every summer evening.**

> Clearly, there are all kinds of possible answers here. The use of **could** emphasizes the possibility, what they *would be able* to do if...

35 **If Mark and Laura slept more, they wouldn't be so tired.**

36 **If I went to the police, I might have to go to court (to give evidence).**

> This sentence might have been difficult. The use of **might** indicates that the person is reluctant to go to the police as he/she doesn't like the idea of going to court.

37 **If you learnt to drive, you could go out a lot more than you do.**

> **Could** expresses the possibility. It is exactly the same as saying *"you would be able to..."*.

38 **If I married a Chinese man/girl, I'd live in China.**

> Again, **would** indicates that your mind is decided. You could use **could** in this sentence, in which case you would be expressing only the possibility rather than the intention.

THE SECOND CONDITIONAL

39 **If I were them, I'd wait for the moment.**

40 **If I was/became President/Prime Minister, I would give more tax breaks to small businesses.**

Seeing your answers to this one would make very interesting reading!

TRACK THREE

Now listen to Track Three on the CD.

SUMMARY

Now you can reflect on what you have learnt about the **Second Conditional** with some further examples.

We have seen how the **Second Conditional** has the following classic or common structure:

If + Past Simple + Conditional (would do)

You'd have more chance of getting a job if you looked in the city.
If she ever saw him again, she'd cry with joy.

We have also seen how **would** can be replaced by a different modal verb.

If + Past Simple + Modal Verb

If a leading publisher saw your work, they might want to publish it.
If Susan lived in France, she could really perfect her French.

Here is a breakdown of the major uses of the **Second Conditional**:

IMAGINARY THINGS

You could eat spicy food as often as you wanted if you lived in Korea.

Your parents could retire and go and live somewhere in the sun if they sold their business now.

If John wasn't so stubborn, he'd accept his wife's suggestion.

I'd watch the late night politics programme every day if I didn't have to get up early for work in the morning.

If I had a car, I'd drive to work.

We wouldn't go back to that hotel (even) if you paid us!

If she used the computer less, she wouldn't get so many headaches.

THE SECOND CONDITIONAL

IMPOSSIBLE THINGS

I'd fly to where you are right now if I had wings.

If we could travel in time, I'd go back to the 1960s.

If you had three sisters, you'd understand my stress.

ADVICE

If you were me, what would you do?

If I were you, I'd write a letter to him first and wait for his response.

I'd ask your boss for a pay rise if I were you.

I'd study Italian, if I were him – it'll be difficult living in Rome without being able to speak the language.

So the **Second Conditional** always deals with events of varying probability - from impossible to unlikely to possible. Its use therefore always relates to the imaginary world.

TRACK FOUR

Now listen to Track Four on the CD.

THE THIRD CONDITIONAL

Like the **Second Conditional**, the **Third Conditional** talks about the imaginary world. It is the easiest of the three **Conditionals** to understand theoretically, but it is the most difficult to form.

The idea of it is easy. The **Third Conditional** always talks about a past action and the consequence of that action. The formation is difficult because the two tenses you need both use an auxiliary verb and a past participle.

The **Third Conditional** deals with the imaginary world, because it imagines the opposite action and the opposite result of a real, past situation.

The classic structure of the **Third Conditional** is:

If + Past Perfect + Conditional Perfect (would have done)

As with the other two **Conditionals**, have a look at the following ten sentences using this structure and think about the meaning and context. You should be getting used to this approach by now.

1   **If my parents hadn't seen the advert, they would never have gone to Russia.**

2   **If Rooney had played, England would've won.**

3   **We wouldn't have bought the house if there hadn't been a tennis club within the vicinity.**

4   **I would've had a big problem if I hadn't had my credit card on me at the time.**

5 If we had gone to the party, we wouldn't have arrived at the office on time this morning.

6 If you hadn't been brave enough to give up your job and start your own business, we'd never have been able to buy a vacation home in Florida.

7 If you'd seen the race, you would've been so nervous.

8 If we'd known that Steve and Melissa had broken off their engagement, naturally we'd never have asked Steve's mum about wedding presents. We felt terrible.

9 I would've been furious if I'd been there.

10 We wouldn't have sent our son to that school if we'd known about the drugs problem there.

The **Third Conditional** talks about a past action/situation, and a past result of that action/situation. The sentence actually then imagines the opposite action and the opposite result.

Have a look now at my explanations of what the ten sentences mean. After the first couple, you will get the idea if you don't understand already.

1 If my parents hadn't seen the advert, they would never have gone to Russia.

Reality: My parents saw the advert, and they did go to Russia.

2 If Rooney had played, England would've won.

Reality: Rooney didn't play and England didn't win.

3 We wouldn't have bought the house if there hadn't been a tennis club within the vicinity.

Reality: There was a tennis club in the vicinity and we did buy the house.

4   **I would've had a big problem if I hadn't had my credit card on me.**

Reality: Luckily I had my credit card on me.

5   **If we had gone to the party, we wouldn't have arrived at the office on time this morning.**

Reality: We didn't go to the party, and therefore we did arrive at the office on time.

6   **If you hadn't been brave enough to give up your job and start your own business, we'd never have been able to buy a vacation home in Florida.**

Reality: You were brave enough to give up your job in order to start your own business, it has been successful, and as a result we have been able to buy a holiday home in Florida.

7   **If you'd seen the race, you would've been so nervous.**

Reality: You didn't see the race.
(The context of this sentence is probably that you had bet a lot of money on the outcome of the race, and it was very close, making it a nervous experience as you waited to see if your horse was going to win or not. Of course, this sentence does not mean that you were not nervous because you didn't see the race. Clearly from this sentence the race was dramatic and close.)

8   **If we'd known that Steve and Melissa had broken off their engagement, naturally we'd never have asked Steve's mum about wedding presents. We felt terrible.**

Reality: We made the unfortunate and embarrassing mistake of asking Steve's mum about wedding presents, because we didn't know that the engagement was off.

9   **I would've been furious if I'd been there.**

Reality: I wasn't there, so there was nothing to make me furious!

10   **We wouldn't have sent our son to that school if we'd known about the drugs problem there.**

Reality: We didn't know about the drugs problem, so we did send our son to that school.

THE THIRD CONDITIONAL

Notice how each sentence talks about a real action/event that has already happened.

The sentences are set in the imaginary world because they imagine the opposite action and the opposite result to something that has already taken place.

SEE APPENDIX TEN

Notice the varied use of the contraction - sometimes it is used, sometimes it is not.

SEE APPENDIX ELEVEN

▼ You have seen how the **Third Conditional** is often used to express either *relief* or *regret*. Have a look at another batch of ten sentences, all of which express one of these two emotions.

Some of the sentences deviate from the classic structure you have learnt by replacing **would** with another modal verb. You have already seen how **will** and **would**, in the **First** and **Second Conditionals** respectively, are sometimes replaced by other modal verbs.

Some notes are given at times to help you understand the context.

11 **If you'd driven, you might've been involved in that pile-up on the highway.**

The sense here is great *relief*, you didn't drive (you went to wherever you were going by another means of transport) and therefore were not on the road at the time of the accident and subsequent pile-up on the highway.

12 **I'd never have gone to Peru for that year if I'd known that you'd meet someone else while I was away.**

Don't be confused by the "**you'd** meet" in this sentence. It is part of the "if I'd known" clause and is used here as the past of

will. It is not part of the **Conditional** structure (i.e. If + Past Perfect + Conditional Perfect.)

The **Conditional** structure is "If I'd known" and "**I'd never** have gone".

Notice the use of "**I'd never**" here, instead of just **wouldn't**. **Would never** emphasizes strongly the speaker's *regret*. It's like saying "There is no way I **would** have gone if I had known...". Have a look back at sentence 6 in this Module which also uses **would never**.

13 **We wouldn't have met each other if you hadn't crashed your bike into my front gate!**

> *Relief* or *regret*? Again, without the context we can't be completely sure, although relief or happiness seems more likely to me. Perhaps that strange event, i.e. someone crashing their bicycle into someone else's front gate, was the beginning of a special friendship between the two people. Sounds like something out of Hollywood, doesn't it?

14 **Isabel would've passed the exam if she hadn't been ill on the day.**

15 **If the paramedics had got here five minutes earlier, they could've saved Simon's life.**

16 **If that man hadn't stopped to give us a lift, we might not have got home tonight.**

> In other words, we might have had to stay in a hotel or a B&B.

17 **James wouldn't have married Chloe if he'd known about her secret problem with the bottle.**

> If you haven't worked it out, a "problem with the bottle" refers to a problem with alcohol.

18 **We'd have been bored to death if we hadn't brought anything to read.**

> "Bored to death" means very, very bored!

19 **Philip and Monica wouldn't have employed Jack as their gardener if they'd known he was a thief.**

Pretty obvious.

20 **If I'd paid the money into my account yesterday, I wouldn't have missed the mortgage repayment.**

Three sentences here move away from the classic structure. Sentences 11 and 16 use **might** instead of **would**, while sentence 15 uses **could**.

▼ Sentences 21-30 give further examples of modal verbs replacing the classic **would** in **Third Conditional** sentences. As with the use of modal verbs in the **First** and **Second Conditionals**, you need to think about how the meaning is altered through their use.

21 **I could've told you the answer if you'd asked me.**

Could here expresses the speaker's ability to have helped.

22 **If we'd had enough time, we could've visited the Great Wall of China.**

Emphasizes the possibility.

23 **Climbing this mountain might have been dangerous if we hadn't had those new boots.**

Here **would** could be used to express a greater certainty of the speaker's opinion. **Might** expresses the possibility.

24 **Tom Cruise was in Harrods this afternoon. If we'd gone there, we might've seen him!**

The use of **might** is correct because it is not certain that we would have seen him, even if we had been there. We might've been there at a different time, or we might have been on another floor to him – there are many reasons why we might

THE THIRD CONDITIONAL

not have seen him. In fact, it is quite unlikely that we would've been in the same place at the same time as him. But clearly the speaker would have wanted to see him, so the use of **might** is 'wishful' – listen to the intonation on the CD.

25 **We might not have arrived on time if we'd come by car – there are some traffic jams because of the demonstrations.**

26 **I couldn't have passed my driving test if you hadn't given me so much of your time to let me practise with you.**

This means exactly the same as "I wouldn't have been able to pass...".

27 **You could've played tennis every day if you'd come with us – there was a grass court in the grounds of the hotel.**

28 **If I hadn't won that money I couldn't have gone on the trip to Brazil.**

This means exactly the same as "I wouldn't have been able to go...".

29 **We may not have heard the alarm if you hadn't left the door open.**

May is sometimes used with the same meaning as **might**. In other words, it relates to *possibility*. It is certainly much more usual to hear **might**, but it is worth giving one example with **may** as sometimes you will hear it used.

30 **I think my mum might've had a heart attack if she'd seen that movie last night.**

Obviously a tense, frightening movie, but the speaker is suggesting that it would have been especially so for his/her mother (i.e. more than for other people). This means that the speaker in the sentence has access to information that we, without the context, can only guess at. In this case, we can imagine something about the mother's health and/or character.

Now have a go at writing some suitable **Third Conditional** sentences for the following situations, just like you did with the other **Conditionals** in the first two Modules. Underneath you can see my suggested answers together with some added notes where appropriate.

It's important for you to check your answers with a native speaker if possible.

1. Yesterday you really wanted to go to the disco but had to baby-sit for your sister. (Sentence 31)

2. James was hoping to go to London last weekend by car, but it broke down on Friday afternoon. (Sentence 32)

3. You didn't revise for your Italian exam at all because you thought you had no chance of passing, but when you took the exam it was easier than you expected and you only narrowly failed. (Sentence 33)

4. Mike's parents were shocked after watching the violent film. (Sentence 34)

5. While spending a year travelling around Europe your friend became very ill. Your family didn't tell you because they didn't want you to worry. (Sentence 35)

6. Sarah went out last night at 7pm and her boyfriend called her ten minutes later, so they couldn't talk to each other. (Sentence 36)

7. John was thinking about (but hadn't fixed his plan) going to Las Vegas for the weekend, but decided not to after catching a cold. (Sentence 37)

8. Julie and Sam decided to get divorced because Sam refused to get help for his snoring problem. (Sentence 38)

9. We took a taxi to the town centre from our house, and it proved to be a good decision as it suddenly poured with rain. (Sentence 39)

10. Claire decided to write a children's book because her grandchildren loved the stories she told so much. (Sentence 40)

SUGGESTED ANSWERS

31 **If I hadn't had to baby-sit for my sister last night, I would've gone to the club.**

32 **If James' car hadn't broken down he would've used it to go to London.**

> Be careful here. We do not know from this sentence that James didn't go to London, we only know that he didn't go in his car. Because it broke down, he would have had to use another means of getting there.

33 **If I'd revised for the Italian exam, I would've passed it.**

> You could have used **might** here, although because he only narrowly failed anyway we can be pretty sure that if he had revised for it he would have passed.

34 **If Mike's parents hadn't seen the film, they wouldn't have been shocked.**

35 **If I'd known my friend was ill, I would've come home to visit him.**

36 **If Sarah had gone out a few minutes later, she could've talked to her boyfriend.**

> Clearly there are lots of **Third Conditional** sentences that could be drawn from this situation. For example, you could have focused on the possibility of him calling earlier, rather than her going out later.

37 **John might've gone to Las Vegas if he hadn't caught a cold.**

> **Might** is the best modal to use here, because the situation tells us that he was thinking about going to Las Vegas. That means he was undecided. Even if he hadn't caught a cold, he still might not have gone.

THE THIRD CONDITIONAL

38 If Sam hadn't refused to get help for his snoring problem, he and Julie wouldn't have decided to get divorced.

39 We would've gotten soaked if we hadn't taken a taxi.

40 If her grandchildren hadn't loved her stories so much, she wouldn't have decided to write the book.

TRACK FIVE

Now listen to Track Five on the CD.

SUMMARY

To finish with, have a look at some more example **Third Conditional** sentences. Try saying the sentences aloud to yourself, become immersed in the structure and the feel of them.

We have seen how the **Third Conditional** has the following classic or common structure:

If + Past Perfect + Conditional Perfect (would have done)

If you'd seen the film with us, you'd have enjoyed it more.

They would've complained if the company hadn't offered them the free cruise as compensation.

I would've swum in the sea every day if I'd been with you last week in Hawaii.

My friends wouldn't have come if they hadn't wanted to.

If I'd known she was upset, I would've talked to her.

We have also seen how **would** can be replaced by a different modal verb in the second part of the sentence

If + Past Perfect + Conditional Perfect (could/might/may have done)

Tyson could've won the fight if he'd been fully fit.

If you hadn't come at that moment, I might've lost my temper completely.

John might not have forgiven his wife if he'd known that it wasn't her first affair.

She could've got that job if her father had let her have the interview.

If you hadn't been so rude to your boss, you might've got promotion.

Here is a breakdown of the major uses of the **Third Conditional**:

REGRET

My life could've been so different if I'd studied hard at school.

If I'd known that Maria wasn't going to the party, I wouldn't have gone either.

If we'd learnt Japanese, we'd have had a much richer experience living in Tokyo.

Simon and Brian wouldn't have been so ill during the night if they hadn't drunk so much in the restaurant.

If you'd waited to sell your house, you could've got a lot more for it.

RELIEF

If you hadn't seen that documentary on the dangers of smoking, you'd never have quit.

I would've eaten that if you hadn't told me there was meat in it!

We wouldn't have gone to the concert if you hadn't recommended it.

My parents would've grounded me if I hadn't passed the exam.

Sarah would've been miserable if she'd married Kevin.

So the **Third Conditional** always imagines opposite actions and outcomes to real events that have happened. Its use therefore always relates to the imaginary world.

TRACK SIX

Now listen to Track Six on the CD.

OTHER CONDITIONALS

The reason that **Conditional** sentences in English are so important is because they are used so frequently. The purpose of Part One has been to deal extensively with them. Hopefully the theory of the three different types of **Conditional** sentences is now clear (or at least clearer) to you.

In this Module we are going to look at some other types of **Conditional** sentence. Firstly though, let's just recap what we've covered in the first three Modules by comparing one sentence expressed in the three classic **Conditional** structures. Have a look at sentences 1-3 with the notes:

1   **If Paul studies, he'll pass the exam.**

A straightforward prediction.

2   **If Paul studied, he'd pass the exam.**

The focus here is on the fact that Paul is not studying at the moment. The speaker affirms his/her confidence in Paul's ability to pass, but a change of attitude is required.

3   **If Paul had studied, he would've passed the exam.**

Three facts are immediately known here: The exam is in the past, Paul didn't study for it, and consequently he failed it.

These three sentences show the essential nature of the **First**, **Second** and **Third Conditionals**, with which you should now be familiar.

Now let's have a look at a new **Conditional** structure, less common than the other three, but nevertheless important to know about. It's the **Zero Conditional**. Look at its structure:

STUCTURE: If + Present Simple + Present Simple

It is often used to express something that is a natural result. Have a look at sentences 4 and 5:

4   **If you put wood on water, it floats.**

5   **If you heat iron to 1500 degrees centigrade, it melts.**

IMPORTANT

1.   Both sentences express something that can be proved by experiment.

The **Zero Conditional** is often used to express scientific facts, where the result is absolutely certain and depends only on the doing of the first action (i.e. putting the wood on the water and heating the iron). The result then follows as surely as night follows day.

2.   In the **Zero Conditional**, the use of "if" carries the same meaning as "when".

This is because the result is certain. Can you see how in both these examples the meaning of the sentence would be exactly the same if the word "when" was used instead of the word "if"?

The second main use of the **Zero Conditional** is to talk about habits in everyday life. Again, the word "if" could perfectly well be replaced by "when" without the sense of the sentence changing at all. Have a look at sentences 6-8 with the notes:

6   **If my ex-wife sees me in the street, she always crosses the road.**

She doesn't want to talk to me.

7   **If I go to a Japanese restaurant, I usually order sushi.**

Obviously my favourite Japanese food.

OTHER CONDITIONALS

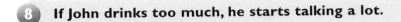

8 **If John drinks too much, he starts talking a lot.**

John suffers from one of the common effects of drinking too much (alcohol).

 IMPORTANT

1.   Often a frequency adverb is used in these types of sentence.

Frequency adverbs tell us how often something is done. The words "always" (sentence 1) and "usually" in sentence 2 are examples of frequency adverbs. They reinforce the habitual nature of things we do/don't do.

2.   The Zero Conditional - like the First Conditional – talks about the real world.

In other words, both deal with real possibilities, things that actually happen or could happen. Look at the **Zero Conditional** example sentences again and see how they are referring to the real world.

Back in Module Two we looked at a particular **Second Conditional** structure used to offer advice ("If I were you, I'd..."). The speaker imagines himself/herself to be in the other person's situation.

A similar kind of sentence can be used with a **Third Conditional** structure:

9 **If I'd been you, I would've hit him.**

Here, the situation is already passed. The speaker (let's call him Sam), having heard from his friend Stuart about what happened, is imagining what he would have done if he had been in that same situation.

SEE APPENDIX TWELVE

There is another way that you can imagine yourself to have been in someone else's situation:

OTHER CONDITIONALS

OTHER CONDITIONALS

10 **If it'd been me, I wouldn't have been so lenient.**

"If it had been me" carries the implicit meaning "*in that situation*". The only difference between "If it had been me" and "If I had been you" is that the latter only imagines myself in *your* situation (i.e. the person the speaker is addressing). The former can be used to imagine myself being in either your situation, or another person's situation.

So the context of sentence 10 could be that you and I are both teachers, and I am comparing something *you did* with what *I would have done*, and I am effectively expressing my opinion that you were not strict enough.

But equally, I could be comparing myself with another teacher, and simply expressing my opinion *to you*.

▼ It's also possible to imagine a situation through someone else's eyes:

11 **If it'd been Dad, he would've been furious.**

SEE APPENDIX THIRTEEN

Let's move on and talk about **Mixed Conditionals**. **Mixed Conditionals** 'mix up' the classic structures that you have learnt to create a nuance of focus. We're going to consider two very important types here. The first type has the following structure:

If + Past Perfect + Conditional (would do)

This is a mixture of the **Second** and **Third Conditionals**. The past perfect is from the **Third Conditional**, and the conditional tense is from the **Second Conditional**. It is almost a **Third Conditional** sentence, the only difference is that instead of using "would have done", just "would do" is used.

Have a look at the following **Mixed Conditional** sentence. In brackets underneath I have put the 'pure' **Third Conditional** sentence, so that you can compare them and think about that slight change of focus/meaning.

12 **If I hadn't drunk so much whiskey last night I wouldn't have a headache.**

(If I hadn't drunk so much whiskey last night I wouldn't have had a headache today.)

How did you get on?

Have a look at two further examples : Sentence 14 again has the equivalent **Third Conditional** sentence in brackets. It is often through comparison of different types of sentence that you can understand the difference. Read the notes too to check your comprehension:

13 **Bernie would be a rich man if he hadn't gambled so much.**

The speaker knows Bernie has had money, but has lost a lot gambling.

14 **If I hadn't gone to that conference in Mexico City, you wouldn't be my wife today.**

(If I hadn't gone to that conference in Mexico City, you would never have become my wife.)

The speaker reflects on the fact that he met his future wife at a conference in Mexico City. He wouldn't have met her if he hadn't gone to that particular conference.

SEE APPENDIX FOURTEEN

▼ The second type of **Mixed Conditional** we are going to look at has the following structure:

If + Past Simple + Conditional Perfect (would have done)

OTHER CONDITIONALS

You have probably spotted immediately that this is again a mix of the **Second** and **Third Conditionals**, but this time we have taken the first part of the **Second Conditional** (the past simple) and combined it with the second part of the **Third Conditional** (the conditional perfect).

Have a look at sentences 15-17 with the explanatory notes:

15 **If I was married, I wouldn't have had dinner with you tonight.**

Susan is suddenly worried that the man she has just met and had dinner with might be married. He assures her that he is not married, and that's why he doesn't feel guilty about having dinner with her (i.e. he has no reason to feel guilty). The sentence indirectly affirms the speaker's moral integrity (i.e. "I wouldn't do that!")

16 **If Bill had a girlfriend, he would've told us.**

We are discussing whether Bill has a girlfriend or not. This sentence concludes that he hasn't, because knowing Bill as we know him, we are sure he wouldn't hide a fact like that (i.e. he would have told us already.)

17 **Martin would've said if he wasn't confident about the investment.**

The speaker's conclusion is that Martin is confident about the investment.

IMPORTANT

Each of these sentences could be expressed with a pure **Third Conditional** structure. As we have already considered, when a **Mixed Conditional** is used instead of one of the classic types, a slight change of focus is introduced by the speaker. What is that change here?

In these three sentences, the focus of the "if" clause is not on a past situation but a present one. "If I was married" (sentence 15), but I'm not (now), "If Bill had a girlfriend" (sentence 16), *but he doesn't* (now), "If he wasn't confident" (sentence 17), *but he is* (now).

Of course, none of the sentences express certainties. The speaker in sentence 15 could be lying, the opinion about Bill expressed in sentence 16 could be wrong, and Martin might only be pretending to be confident about the investment in sentence 17.

The point about these sentences is that they are used to draw conclusions about the present reality.

Quite often continuous tenses are used in **Conditional** sentences. Look at the following structure:

If + Present Continuous + Future (will do / going to do)

This is a spin-off of the **First Conditional**. Instead of the Present Simple being used, the Present Continuous is used. Have a look at two example sentences and their suggested contexts. The notes will help you to understand:

18 **If your Spanish students are coming to the party, I'll make some sangria.**

Sean is having a party, and his friend Pamela has a couple of Spanish students living with her at the moment. They have discussed the possibility of the students coming to the party, and it seems likely that they will. The use of the continuous tense makes it sound much more probable (indeed, almost certain) that the students will come.

19 **If you're not studying tonight, we could go out.**

Alan feels like spending some time with his girlfriend, Esther. The use of the Present Continuous tells us clearly that Esther has already said that she isn't going to study tonight. So, Alan makes his suggestion.

 **IMPORTANT**

The use of the continuous tense in the **First Conditional** usually means that something has already been discussed or considered. Information is known to the speaker, and that's why what is expressed is (usually) much more than just a possibility. It becomes quite likely (as is suggested in sentence 18) or virtually certain (as in sentence 19).

OTHER CONDITIONALS

Now have a look at the structure used when a continuous tense is used in the **Second Conditional**:

| **If + Past Continuous + Conditional (would do)**

Instead of the Past Simple being used, the Past Continuous is used. Have a look at two example sentences, bearing in mind what you know about what the **Second Conditional** is used for:

20 **If you weren't working so much at the moment, you could spend more time with your kids.**

21 **I know you don't like the fact that I'm writing a book about sex. If I was writing a book about volcanoes, you wouldn't complain.**

 IMPORTANT

The **Second Conditional** imagines something that is not real at the moment. So the meaning of sentence 20 (sounds like a wife's words to her husband) is that he is working *very much at the moment* and therefore doesn't have much time to spend with his kids.

Likewise in sentence 21, the reality is that the speaker is not writing a book about volcanoes. The given context makes it clear that the person being spoken to is not happy about the subject matter of the speaker's book.

The use of the Past Continuous, as opposed to the Past Simple, focuses on the ongoing nature of the activity (i.e. *working very much and writing a book*).

Now have a look at the structure used when a continuous tense is used in the **Third Conditional**:

| **If + Past Perfect Continuous + Conditional Perfect (would have done)**

Instead of the Past Perfect being used, the Past Perfect Continuous is used. Remember what the **Third Conditional** is used for, and have a look at sentences 22 and 23:

OTHER CONDITIONALS

22 **If the children hadn't been playing outside for so long yesterday, they wouldn't have caught colds.**

23 **Climbing this mountain might've been dangerous if we hadn't been wearing those new boots.**

Sentence 23 can be found in Module Three (also number 23) as a classic **Third Conditional** sentence.

 IMPORTANT

Just as with the classic **Third Conditional**, these sentences are talking about something that has already happened.

The opposite actions and the opposite results are imagined. The only difference is that the action is described in a continuous way, i.e. the children *were playing* outside yesterday for a long time (sentence 22), and we *were wearing* those boots while climbing the mountain (sentence 23).

The speaker, by using a continuous tense, focuses on the duration of the activity.

Have a look at one further example and the notes:

24 **If we'd been listening to the radio attentively, we would've heard the weather warnings and not got stuck.**

The speaker is regretting that we were not listening to the radio more carefully while driving. He is focusing on the *continuous period of time of not listening carefully*, which has resulted in them getting stuck.

The sense of the **First, Second** and **Third Conditionals** remains the same when they use a continuous tense. The **First Conditional** continues to talk about the real world, and the **Second** and **Third Conditionals** continue to relate to the imaginary world.

Occasionally, the Present Perfect tense can be used in the "if" clause of a **Conditional** sentence. Have a look at this new structure:

OTHER CONDITIONALS

If + Present perfect + Future (will or going to)

Sentences with this structure are another spin-off from the **First Conditional**, because they talk about the real world. Have a look at sentences 25 and 26:

25 **If you haven't written that letter to Uncle Nigel by the time I get back from the shops, I'll be very angry.**

26 **If the builders haven't finished the work on my house by the end of next week, I'm going to deduct 10% from their bill.**

Both sentences give a *time limit* on something being done, and outline a threat if their request is not fulfilled. The Present Perfect can be used in this way when the action being described *has to be completed by a certain time.*

The Passive voice is also sometimes used in **Conditional** sentences. Have a look at sentences 27 and 28. For each of them, the equivalent active sentence is written in brackets:

27 **The company will go bankrupt if no investors are found.**

(If the company can't find any investors, the company will go bankrupt.)

28 **If the government doesn't pay the ransom by Friday, the hostages will be killed.**

(If the government doesn't pay the ransom by Friday, the kidnappers will kill the hostages.)

To finish with, have a look at an unusual – but important - **Conditional** sentence type. One very common mistake that a lot of students make when they use **Conditional** sentences is to put "would" in the "if" clause (i.e. "If I would..."). That is never right. Well, almost never. Have a look at our last two sentences with the notes:

48

29 **If you'd like to come this way, I'll take you through to Mr. McIvor's office.**

The speaker is probably Mr. McIvor's secretary, and is addressing someone who has an appointment with him. "If you'd like" is a polite way of telling someone what they should do next, in a formal situation. (Here, it's like a polite, "Follow me".)

30 **If you'd all like to take a seat now, the show can begin.**

The speaker is addressing a group of people, and is politely instructing them that it is time to take their seats. This type of sentence is always polite, and is reserved for business and formal situations.

> The structure is nearly always "If you would like to...". This is not the same as asking someone, "Would you like to...?". It is more assertive, like making a polite request or indicating a course of action (i.e. "This is what you should do now").

Now have a go at writing some suitable **Conditional** sentences for the following situations, based on the sentence types that you have studied in this Module. You have taken in a lot here, so take your time in thinking about the following situations to find the right sentence type. Underneath you can see some suggested answers.

It's important for you to check your answers with a native speaker if possible.

1. You like drinking and gambling, but your habit is never to do them both at the same time. (Sentence 31)

2. You are a company secretary. The directors have just arrived for a meeting with the Chief Executive. Politely request that they give you their coats and take a seat in the reception for a moment, while you notify your boss of their arrival. (Sentence 32)

3. Your wife has developed a nasty cough because she is smoking a lot at the moment. Point this out to her. (Sentence 33)

4. Remind your parents that at this moment in time they are not in Africa because they rejected the prize of a free holiday in Kenya that they won in a competition. (Sentence 34)

5. Because of studying during the day and working at night, Joel has only been sleeping for three hours a night. Yesterday he fainted during his university class and had to go to hospital for tests. (Sentence 35)

6. Your girlfriend (Rachel) has just met your parents for the first time. After dinner they showed her their wedding photos. Rachel is worried that your parents didn't like her, but you reassure her that the fact they showed her their wedding photos disproves her worries. (Sentence 36)

7. Colin has just told his wife Christine that he is going to watch a basketball match on T.V. tonight. Christine wants to watch a documentary, so she tells Colin that she will go and watch it with their neighbours, who are friends of theirs. (Sentence 37)

8. Your friend tells you about how he saw a fight on the street between two men last night while walking home, but didn't do anything. Tell him what you would have done. (Sentence 38)

9. It's Saturday morning, and you've been waiting in your office for three hours for an important fax that one of your suppliers promised to send you. You are fed up, and call your business partner to tell her that 12.00 is the deadline, after which time you will leave. (Sentence 39)

10. Mark can speak French because he lived in Paris for four years. (Sentence 40)

SUGGESTED ANSWERS

31 If I gamble, I never drink.

32 If you'd each like to hand me your coat, and then take a seat for a moment, I'll let her know that you are here.

33 You wouldn't have that nasty cough if you weren't smoking so much.

OTHER CONDITIONALS

34 If you'd accepted the prize, you'd be in Kenya right now.

35 If Joel had been sleeping enough recently, he wouldn't have fainted in class.

36 Rachel, if they didn't like you, they wouldn't have shown you their wedding photos. That's a very good sign!

37 If you're watching the basketball game tonight, I'll go and watch the documentary with Adrian and Isabel.

38 If it'd been me, I would've called the police.

39 If they haven't sent the fax by 12.00, I'm going home.

40 If Mark hadn't lived in Paris for four years, he wouldn't be able to speak French.

TRACK SEVEN

Now listen to Track Seven on the CD.

SUMMARY

Now you have a chance to see some more examples that will help you to further develop your feel of how these sentence types are used. It is easier to summarize what you have learnt in this Module by structure as opposed to use, which is what I have done.

ZERO CONDITIONALS

If you heat water to 100 degrees centigrade, it boils.

If we don't have to get up early, we usually read the newspaper in bed with a cup of coffee.

My parents aren't adventurous. If they go abroad, they never try any local food.

MIXED CONDITIONALS

If your father hadn't invested in your business from the outset, you wouldn't have a beautiful four-bedroom detached house in the suburbs of Los Angeles to live in.

I'd play football every week if I hadn't injured my knee last year. Now I only play twice a month.

If they were sensible, they would never have paid so much for a one-bedroom flat.

If I didn't love you Nikki, I wouldn't have moved to Colorado to be with you.

CONTINUOUS CONDITIONALS

If you're using the computer this afternoon, I'll clean the office and go to the bank and the post office.

If I were setting up a business, I'd have to take out a bank start-up loan. I haven't got any capital.

If the dogs hadn't been barking, I'm sure the burglars would've come to our house instead of next door.

This morning we would've gone for a walk if it hadn't been raining.

PRESENT PERFECT CONDITIONALS

If I haven't phoned you by midnight, call the police and tell them where I am.

If you haven't finished your homework by the time I get home, I'll call your teacher and ask him to put you in detention.

PASSIVE CONDITIONALS

If nobody claims the car, it will be sold and the money given to charity.

If the staff aren't given a pay rise, they're going to strike.

OTHER

If it'd been me, I wouldn't have asked Matthew to help me.

If I'd been you, I would've asked for more time to think about it.

If it'd been Felix, he would've played on in spite of the injury.

What would you have done if you'd been me?

If you'd like to take a seat in the waiting room, I'll be with you shortly.

TRACK EIGHT

Now listen to Track Eight on the CD.

INTRODUCTION TO PART TWO

Modules 5-8 deal with **Modal Verbs**. You have already seen a lot of **Modal Verbs** in the first four Modules.

Studying conditionals and **Modal Verbs** together is sensible, because they are so often found together. Some of the example sentences here in Part Two are conditional sentences.

You've already got an idea about the uses of **could**, **would** and **might** from Part One. The purpose of Part Two of the book is to further your understanding of them and help you to develop a feel for the other ones.

Modal verbs express varying degrees of possibility, probability and necessity of events or situations.

Have a look at the table below. It outlines which **Modal verbs** are used to express which concepts.

POSSIBILITY	**Can**	**Could**	**Might**
ABILITY	**Can**	**Could**	
PERMISSION	**Can**	**Could**	**Would**
OBLIGATION	**Should**	**Must**	
DEDUCTION	**Can't**	**Must**	**Might**
PROBABILITY	**Might**	**Must**	

Rather than study the **Modal Verbs** by concepts, the second part of this book looks at them in pairs. This is because the concepts often overlap with each other. It doesn't matter if in a particular sentence the use of **could** is possibility or ability (sometimes we can't tell the difference). What matters is that you develop a feel for the sense of each **Modal Verbs**.

This is because – as you can see from the table - **Modal Verbs** are not limited to one particular use. Most of them can be used to express more than one concept.

The best way to become familiar with them is to see / hear them used in many different situations, and thereby develop a feel for how and when they should be used.

Modal Verbs are extremely important in English, because they are so common in spoken and written language. They also convey the feeling or mood of the speaker, often in a subtle way. The intonation is often vital to understanding the feeling behind the words.

Using **modal verbs** in your spoken and written English is imperative for natural and effective communication.

Acquiring - and in time mastering - a comprehension of their meaning and use is what it means to develop a sense of English. It will not only enable you to communicate more efficiently, it will allow you to inject your own personality into your English communication.

THE USES OF CAN AND COULD

First of all, let's consider **can** and **could** in terms of their roots. They both come from the verb 'to be able', and it's therefore logical that they are used to talk about people's ability to do something – whether in the present (**can**), or in the past (**could**).

Have a look at example sentences 1-10 which demonstrate this. Sometimes I have added some notes which paraphrase the meaning of the sentences using either the verb 'to be able' or the noun 'ability'.

1 I could swim from the age of six.

2 Nathan can do the spreadsheets because he knows Excel.

Nathan's ability makes him a suitable person to create the spreadsheets.

3 Can you do your homework without a calculator?

4 Mike could beat anyone on his day.

This doesn't mean that Mike always won, but that his ability was as good as anyone else's and that he was *able* to beat any other player.

5 My father could still play a round of golf when he was seventy six.

In spite of his age, he was still fit and strong enough *to be able* to play golf.

6 Kelly couldn't drive because of her leg, so Steve was stuck behind the wheel all the way to Kansas.

Steve had to do all the driving because Kelly *wasn't able* to do any.

7 **Let's see how many omelettes you can make in the next half-an-hour.**

> A challenge to someone's ability to make omelettes quickly.

8 **My parents couldn't get into the house for an hour because I had taken the key by mistake.**

> My parents *weren't able* to get into the house and had to wait for me for an hour to return to the house with the key.

9 **I went to several shops, but I couldn't find the perfume you wanted.**

10 **A friend of mine can run a kilometre in under three minutes.**

> You can see from these sentences that when **can** and **could** are used to express ability, they mean exactly the same as "is/are able" (**can**) and "was/were able" (**could**).

> So, when **can** and **could** are used to express ability, **can** talks about a present ability and **could** talks about a past ability.

> However, the second major use of **can** and **could** is to express possibility, and when used in this way they don't relate to past and present. We will come back to this point after looking at sentences 11-20, all of which express possibility.

> Again, there are sometimes some additional notes to enable you to be absolutely sure that you have understood the sentences correctly.

11 **My home town can be very wet in April.**

> Sometimes it rains a lot at that time of year in my hometown.

12 **It could be a very close match between Italy and Brazil.**

> Someone suggests that the outcome of this game might be difficult to predict.

13 **Could you meet me in the library at about 7pm?**

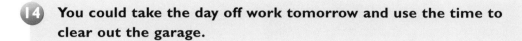

14 **You could take the day off work tomorrow and use the time to clear out the garage.**

A suggestion of a possible course of action.

15 **People can work hard without necessarily earning a lot of money.**

It doesn't follow that working hard will make people rich.

16 **John could be sacked if the boss finds out he was drunk yesterday after coming back from lunch.**

A First Conditional sentence – it shouldn't therefore need any explaining!

17 **It can be difficult to stop smoking.**

18 **My dad can be so stubborn at times!**

19 **The bus that goes downtown from here can be crowded up to 11am.**

20 **We couldn't go to the concert because it was sold out.**

IMPORTANT

1. Notice how **can** is used to talk about a general **possibility** – look at sentences 11, 15, 17, 18 &19.

In each sentence, **can** expresses what is sometimes true. In fact, the sense of **can** as a *general* possibility suggests that something is actually quite often true – in sentence 11, we can imagine that it is quite common for it to rain a lot in the speaker's home town. The sense is the same in the other four sentences that use **can**.

2. Notice how **could** is used for a specific **possibility** – look at the other five sentences.

Each sentence with **could** relates to a particular situation – in sentence 12, the comment relates to one forthcoming match, not to any match between Brazil and Italy. The sense is the same in the other four sentences that use **could**.

The use of **could**, when talking about possibility, is related to a particular situation.

THE USES OF CAN AND COULD

59

SEE APPENDIX FIFTEEN

Intonation can often indicate the speaker's emphasis on one of the two concepts, as opposed to the other.

Have a look at sentences 21 and 22. The written words are identical, but I have italicised different words in each sentence. The italicised words are the words which the speaker will emphasize in the spoken sentence. You will hear this on the CD track at the end of this Module. The sentence is a repeat of a Third Conditional sentence from Module Three:

21 **If the paramedics had got here five minutes earlier, *they* could've saved Simon's life.**

22 **If the paramedics had got here five minutes earlier, they *could've* saved Simon's life.**

In sentence 21, the emphasis is on they, which emphasizes the ability of the paramedics. In other words, the speaker's belief that Sam's life could have been saved is based on his confidence in the paramedics' ability. Emphasizing the person has the effect of highlighting ability.

We don't have the context for this sentence, but it's possible that the confidence expressed by the speaker in the paramedics' ability is *as opposed to* another person's ability. Perhaps the situation is that someone else tried and failed to save Simon while waiting for the paramedics to arrive. The sentence is then a comparison.

In contrast, sentence 22 emphasizes the possibility of Simon's life having been saved. Of course this is totally connected to the paramedics' ability, but...

The emphasis on **could** (instead of on *they*) implies that the outcome of the situation depended on other factors as well, making it impossible to state that, without any doubt, Simon's life would have been saved. Therefore what is being emphasized is the possibility (i.e. maybe he could have been saved, but maybe not.)

In this sense, sentence 21 is a more definite statement, i.e. the speaker is more sure. He/She is not emphasizing possibility.

SEE APPENDIX SIXTEEN

Have a look at another similar example in sentences 23 and 24, this time using **can**.

23 **You *can* climb to the top of the mountain and return in a day.**

24 **You can climb to the top of the mountain and return in a day.**

Remember how **can** is used to express general possibilities? That is the case in sentence 23. "You can climb" is impersonal, it is not referring to a specific person. It is the same as saying "one can climb" or "it is possible to climb".

Sentence 24 on the other hand is totally personal – emphasizing a particular person's ability to climb the mountain, based on their strength and fitness.

Listen carefully to the two sentences on the CD later and try and pick up on the nuance of emphasis and the effect it creates.

Can and **Could** are also used to ask for and give permission to do something.

Have a look at sentences 25-28:

25 **Could I invite my friends over tomorrow?**

Asking permission.

26 **Can I smoke in here?**

Asking permission.

27 **Of course you can use my cell phone!**

Giving permission.

28 **You can watch the film with me if you promise to go straight to bed when it is finished.**

Giving permission (a First Conditional sentence).

Permission can also be refused using **can** and **could**. Look at sentences 29-31. There are notes to help you.

29 **You can't make any phone calls tonight because you've got a lot of homework to do.**

An example of permission being denied.

30 **When I was in the army, we couldn't watch TV at all during the week.**

Unlike in sentence 29, the denial of permission here is indirect. **Couldn't** here means exactly the same as "weren't allowed to watch" – it therefore relates to rules and regulations (here, a refusal of permission).

31 **The boundaries for the game are the grounds of the house – you can't go outside the gates.**

Again, the denial of permission is indirect because no one is specifically asking to go outside the grounds of the house. This sentence is a statement of a rule - refusing permission.

Can and **could** are also used to ask for help and favours, as in sentences 32 and 33:

32 **Can you help me with my geography homework?**

33 **Could you do me a favour? Could you pick up some shampoo for me when you go to the supermarket?**

IMPORTANT

When **can** and **could** are used in question sentences, **could** is generally formal and polite, although it can be used with an informal intonation amongst friends and those close to you. **Can** is exclusively informal and suitable for use amongst friends and people of the same age.

Another very important use of **could** is to make suggestions. You have already seen this in some Conditional sentences in Module One.

Have a look at the sentences 34-38 which all make suggestions:

34 **We could try out that new American restaurant tomorrow night if you like.**

35 **I could pick up the children from school on the way back from the dentist.**

36 **I told my parents they could stay with me for the night but dad insisted on driving home in spite of the snow.**

37 **You could write a book about all your adventures travelling in Asia for a year.**

38 **We could take the night train and save money on paying for a hotel.**

 IMPORTANT

I. Notice how all these sentences express **possibility**.

The nature of a suggestion is that it talks about a possible future course of action. We have already made the point about possibility being connected to the future - a suggestion (at the time of making it) is also a possibility.

The only exception to that here is sentence 36, where the speaker is referring to a past situation. He/She explains how a suggestion of his/hers was rejected by his/her dad.

2. The use of **could** to suggest a course of action usually demands a response.

In this sense it is like asking a question, and in fact a suggestion with **could** is often followed by something like "What do you think?" or "if you like", as in sentence 34.

63

Finally, we need to make brief mention here of another **modal verb**. **May** is not an important **modal verb** in modern day English – it is used far less nowadays than it used to be. Its most important use is probably to name the month that comes after April! It does need a mention as a **modal verb** though, as you will come across it from time to time.

I include it briefly at this point because it relates to two of the concepts we have considered in this Module – permission and possibility.

Here we are going to look at it expressing permission. In Module Seven it is mentioned briefly again in its capacity to express possibility.

Have a look at sentences 39 and 40:

39 **May I come in?**

40 **May I see the photos of John?**

The use of **may** to ask permission is extremely formal. Extremely, extremely formal. The reality is that it is so formal that there are very few situations serious enough to warrant its use.

Even when I imagine the most formal situation I can, like for example, having tea with the queen of England, it does not occur to me (as a native speaker) to use the word **may** to show courtesy.

If I needed to use the bathroom in Buckingham Palace (the London home of the Queen of England) for example, I would construct a sentence of permission using **would**. In modern day English, **would** can be used to express an adequate level of courtesy for any situation.

SEE APPENDIX SEVENTEEN

Now it's your turn to try and imagine some suitable sentences using **can** and **could** for the situations below.

As with the other exercises, there are no fixed answers here, so I have given some possible answers underneath, and some added explanatory notes where appropriate.

It is important that you check your answers with a native speaker to see if the answers you come up with are suitable or not.

1. You learnt how to ski when you were ten. (Sentence 41)

2. You had planned to go to a disco tomorrow night with your friend, but you have heard that your ex-girlfriend is going to go and you don't want to meet her. Suggest an alternative plan to your friend, either for tomorrow night or another occasion. (Sentence 42)

3. Tell your friend something that is generally true about people from your country. (Sentence 43)

4. Ask your neighbour to do you the favour of lending you his guidebook of Italy as you are going there next week. (Sentence 44)

5. Tell your friend that you have heard a very cold winter has been predicted by some weather experts. (Sentence 45)

6. Explain to your mum that it's not permitted to use the communal swimming pool at the holiday complex in Tenerife where you are staying after 8.30pm. (Sentence 46)

7. Ask your friend John to take you to the airport for your trip to Canada next week. (Sentence 47)

8. Give your opinion about which city would be suitable to host the next Olympic Games, and give a reason. (Sentence 48)

9. Give your son permission to go to his friend's party tomorrow night provided he returns home by midnight. (Sentence 49)

10. Sue, a work colleague of yours, has looked so happy lately, but you don't know why. Suggest a possible reason to another colleague. (Sentence 50)

THE USES OF CAN AND COULD

SUGGESTED ANSWERS

41 I could ski from the age of ten.

42 We could go out for a quiet drink somewhere instead, and we could go to the disco next week.

43 Spanish people can be very unpunctual!

44 Could you do me a favour? Could you lend me your guidebook of Italy?

45 They say it could be a really cold winter this year.

46 Mum, you can't use the pool after 8.30pm.

47 Can you take me to the airport on Thursday, John?

48 I think Paris could host the next Olympics – it's a city with a good infrastructure already in place.

49 You can go to the party as long as you are back by 12.00.

50 Sue could be in love!

TRACK NINE

Now listen to Track Nine on the CD.

In the following paragraph there are six gaps which should be filled using either **can** or **could**. Read through the paragraph carefully and decide which of the two is suitable for each gap.

There...(1)...be a storm tonight in Atlanta, coming in from the west. The late summer...(2)...bring stormy weather in this part of the world. Old Joe (who lives out on the plain)...(3)...lose his fence if he doesn't repair it this afternoon. The winds here...(4)...bring down trees that have stood for fifty years. The problem is that old Joe...(5)...be pretty lazy, and he might not get round to fixing that fence, trusting luck as he usually does. Of course, he...(6)...ask one of his neighbours to give him a hand, like me for example.

You can hear the completed paragraph on the CD.

TRACK TEN

Now listen to Track Ten on the CD.

THE USES OF CAN AND COULD

SUMMARY

Now you have a chance to look at further example sentences with **can** and **could** expressing the concepts we have considered in this Module.

Here's a breakdown of their major uses:

ABILITY

I could speak English, Spanish and Italian fluently by the time I left the army.

Susan's brother couldn't ride a bicycle until he was eighteen.

Can you fix my computer for me?

POSSIBILITY / IMPOSSIBILITY

It can be very embarrassing when you are talking to someone you've met before and you can't remember their name.

We couldn't get through to Andrew for half-an-hour because his phone was switched off during the concert.

Ruby couldn't come unfortunately; she isn't well.

PERMISSION

Can I come round to watch the game with you tonight? Joe's got some of her friends coming round.

I couldn't go out at all during the holidays - my parents made me study all day.

You can bring the kids to the reception as long as they behave themselves.

HELP / FAVOURS

Could I borrow your car for about three hours tomorrow afternoon? I've got to pick up some boxes from the warehouse.

Rich, could you give me a hand clearing out the attic sometime? I think a lot of the stuff up there is yours.

Can I ask you a favour? Can you answer the phone if it rings in the next few minutes; I've got to go to the bank.

SUGGESTIONS (COULD)

I could lend you my rucksack for your trip if you want.

We could go to the beach now for an hour while the sun's shining and study later on this afternoon.

You could take Michelle away for a romantic weekend somewhere and try and patch things up.

TRACK ELEVEN

Now listen to Track Eleven on the CD.

You've taken in a lot of information in this Module. Take your time to absorb it by re-reading the text and re-listening to the CD as much as you need to.

A large part of the process of developing 'a sense of English' (or any language) involves regular and repeated exposure. Your sense of the language then develops largely at a sub-conscious level. Immerse yourself in English; listen to the sentences on the CDs and practise saying them to yourself over and over. Imitate the intonation. Practise changing the intonation or emphasis to create different moods and effects. Use a native speaker to help you.

THE USES OF CAN AND COULD

THE USES OF WOULD AND SHOULD

Unlike **can** and **could**, **would** and **should** will be dealt with separately in this Module as they are not used to express the same concepts.

In the introduction to Part Two, you can see that according to our 'concept table' for **modal verbs**, **would** is used in connection with permission.

However, you have already learnt a lot about **would** in Part One. As you know, it is the base **modal verb** used in the classic structures of both the Second and Third Conditionals.

In this Module we will recap some of the things we have already covered about **would**, and also have a look at some new situations in which it is used in English.

SEE APPENDIX EIGHTEEN

Have a look at sentences 1-5. They give examples of the polite use of **would** in asking for permission to do something, or for a favour:

1 **Would you mind if I watched the news?**

2 **Would you be able to do me a favour tomorrow?**

3 **Would your parents mind if we left the car in the garage? Jeff's had some trouble starting it in the mornings in this cold weather.**

4 **Would you be able to drop me at the station tomorrow morning on your way to work? I've got an early start.**

5 **Would you mind if I turned the radio down a bit?**

IMPORTANT

I.   Sentences 1, 3 and 5 use the structure "**Would** you/somebody mind if I/we/somebody did something?"

This is the structure for asking permission using **would**. Notice how the past tense is used: "if I watched" (sentence 1), "if we left" (sentence 3) and "if I turned" (sentence 5). The past tense is always used after this "**Would** you mind if...?" structure.

2.   Sentences 2 and 4 use the structure "**Would** you/someone be able to do something?"

This is the conditional tense of the verb 'to be able'. It is therefore simply a more polite way of saying "Could you/somebody do something?"

Would is also used to make statements of intent. In Module Two you have already seen how this can apply in Second Conditional sentences. Here are a couple of reminders:

6   **My dad would take up golf again if he didn't have a bad back.**

This is a statement of intent. My dad's mind is clear - he knows what he would do. But the sentence belongs to the imaginary world because he is unable to carry out his wish.

7   **My sister would buy a house overlooking the beach if she had enough money.**

The speaker knows his sister well enough to be able to state an intent of hers.

▼   Look at sentences 8-10 which are all further examples of statements of intent in the imaginary world, but which are not Second Conditional sentences. I've added some notes.

8   **I would love to go to Africa.**

Be very clear about the sense of a sentence like this. At the time of speaking, the speaker hasn't got any particular plan to go to Africa. The sentence is purely an expression of a desire that they have.

9 **I wouldn't invest in stocks and shares, I'd be too worried about losing money.**

The statement of intent is the affirmation of what the speaker would not do! They show us a cautious approach and an unwillingness to take risks with their money.

Sometimes this sort of sentence is used as a way of giving advice to someone else who is considering investing (just like the "If I were you I would/wouldn't..." structure you studied in Module Two).

10 **My girlfriend wouldn't move to the East Coast with me, she wants to be near her family.**

Here I am speculating about my girlfriend's response. I haven't asked her yet, but I feel pretty certain about what her answer would be.

Remember that **would** indicates certainty. So from previous conversations with her (maybe through my indirect prompting!) I have realized that she wouldn't be prepared to move away from her family. Of course, because I haven't asked her directly, I can't be absolutely sure, but using **would** in this 'speculative' way conveys that I strongly believe that I already know her mind and intent.

Statements of intent using **would** are not only used for imaginary situations. In reported speech, **would** can be used as the past of will, and those cases belong to the real world.

Consider:

11 **My mum said she'd go to the party.**

This is a specific, real situation. My mum was invited to the party and agreed to go.

That means at some point in the past she said, "I will go." The use of **would** here is to report that past affirmation. Therefore this is the real world.

SEE APPENDIX NINETEEN

Sentences 12-14 also use **would** to express someone's past statement of intent:

(12) You said you'd bring me back some cigars from Cuba – did you?

A promise was made – "I will bring...". We don't know yet whether the promise was fulfilled or not.

(13) Sarah said she'd call me last night, but she didn't.

A promise was made – "I will call...". As opposed to sentence 12, we know for certain that Sarah didn't keep her promise.

(14) Colin and Rachel called about an hour ago to say they'd be late.

A polite course of action to let someone who is expecting them know that "we'll be a bit late".

In each of these last three sentences **would** is being used to report a sentence that was said in the past and that used "will" (or "going to").

You have seen how **would** is used to ask for permission. **Wouldn't** is used in reported speech to express how permission was denied, or someone's refusal to do something.

Consider sentence 15:

(15) Paul wouldn't let me read the letter.

The meaning of this sentence should be clear.
The use of **wouldn't** tells us that permission is being denied. In other words, in this situation, Paul knew that I wanted to read the letter, but he **wouldn't** allow me to do so.

This is the difference between using "**wouldn't**" and a straightforward negative, i.e. "He didn't let me read...".

Wouldn't emphasizes the denial of permission, or a straightforward refusal to do something. In this way it is stronger than saying "didn't".

Sentences 16-19 give further examples, sometimes with notes.

16 **We took the kids to the beach today but they wouldn't go swimming in the sea because they said it was too cold!**

> There is a context to this sentence. It is a specific situation and there is a particular reason why the kids refused to swim, which we know. Without a context however, the sentence could have different meanings. Compare with sentence 17:

17 **The kids wouldn't go swimming in the sea.**

> From this isolated sentence (i.e. no context) we don't know if the meaning is specific (like in sentence 16) or general (like in, for example, sentence 9). There is no context to tell us if the sentence relates to a particular occasion or whether it is a general comment expressing how the kids always refuse to go swimming (regardless of the day, or the temperature of the water, or any other factors).

18 **My brother wouldn't lend me any money, so I had to use my credit card.**

> This is a specific situation. The use of the past tense ("so I had to use...") places the situation firmly in the real world.

19 **Our dog Rusty wouldn't eat his dinner so we took him to the vet.**

> Now look at sentence 20, which is the same as sentence 10 except for one small – but very important – difference.

20 **My girlfriend wouldn't move to the East Coast with me, she wanted to be near her family.**

> You will remember that sentence 10 was speculative. Here in sentence 20 a past tense is used, "she wanted", instead of "she wants", which makes the situation specific. The meaning here is that I asked my girlfriend to move with me, but she refused. In sentence 10 I was just imagining what her response would be, but I hadn't actually asked her. Here in sentence 20 I have asked, she has refused, and she has confirmed her reason.

▼ **Would** is also used in the sentence structure "I wish somebody/something **would/wouldn't** do something."

Sentences 21-24 give examples of this:

21 **I wish Jules wouldn't hang his wet clothes over the sofa.**

Jules has this bad habit and the speaker is frustrated by it.

22 **We do wish you'd stay for dinner – there's an overload of food.**

The use of "do" just emphasizes how much we wish. Listen to the intonation on the CD at the end of the Module.

23 **I really wish your parents wouldn't smoke in front of the children.**

An annoyed son-in-law or daughter-in-law, probably.

The use of "really" – like the "do" in sentence 22 - is an emphasis. It is fairly common to hear "do wish" or "really wish".

24 **I wish it would snow – it's Christmas day!**

▼ Now let's turn to **should**.

Should is one of the easiest **modal verbs** to understand and to use. Its main function is to give advice and/or impose obligations.

Have a look at the example sentences 25-30:

25 **You shouldn't listen to music while you're studying, Rebecca.**

Often the use of **should** falls between imposing an obligation and giving advice. Here the speaker (let's imagine it's Rebecca's father) might be just giving some advice, he might be insisting that she turns off the music, or his sentence might fall between the two and consequently be unclear. You've guessed it – the intonation would certainly give us an indication. Listen for yourself on the CD and decide what the speaker's mind is.

26 | **I should start getting up earlier in the morning.**

Is this advice or obligation? It seems to me to be more an obligation, as it is self-imposed (i.e. I am telling myself something that I should do).

27 | **You should try and read more; it'll help you to express yourself better in your writing.**

Definitely advice.

28 | **I told your cousins they should visit the Colosseum when they're in Rome.**

Advice again, but here it is more like a recommendation. We can assume that the advice given is based on the personal experience of the speaker when he/she visited the Colosseum.

29 | **Your brother was very rude last night and I want you to tell him that he should say sorry to my mum.**

Here there is a definite sense of obligation. It is advice which really should be taken.

30 | **If John comes back you should leave immediately by the back door. I don't want him to know that you were here.**

Again the sense is an obligation. We can feel that the speaker has the right to ask the person to leave.

IMPORTANT

Should can be said to have expressed an obligation when the advice is delivered strongly. That occurs in the two sentences that mention the word obligation in the notes, i.e. 29 and 30, and also possibly in sentence 25 – depending on what we gauge from the intonation about the speaker's mood.

THE USES OF WOULD AND SHOULD

Should can also be used to express opinions. Have a look at three examples:

31 **Public transport is getting worse and worse. We shouldn't have to wait forty-five minutes for a bus to the town centre.**

i.e. The buses **should** be more frequent.

32 **Burglars who attack people in their own homes should face much harsher sentences.**

i.e. The sentences are far too lenient.

33 **I don't think there should be any single-sex schools at all.**

i.e. Boys and girls **should** have to grow up together; there shouldn't even be a choice.

Sometimes the use of **should** to offer an opinion is akin to making a kind of prediction. Have a look at sentences 34-36, and notice how they all relate to the future.

34 **It should be a good game between the Jets and the Rams.**

The speaker is saying what he thinks will happen.

35 **The shop should still be open to buy the batteries for your camera, but if not we can pick some up at a gas station.**

An alternative plan is suggested if the 'prediction' turns out to be wrong. In the speaker's opinion though, the shop will still be open.

36 **Ryan should pass the exam.**

You have seen this kind of sentence in Module One as the second part of a First Conditional sentence. Here is it simply a prediction/opinion offered by the speaker who obviously knows Ryan and his ability.

We need to make mention of another minor **modal verb** here.

Shall is used for two important things in English - to offer and to suggest. Its use is very easy and clear.

Have a look firstly at sentences 37 and 38:

37 **Shall I help you with your suitcase?**

38 **Shall I take the phone off the hook so that we won't be disturbed?**

The question sentence structure "**Shall** I..." is used to offer to do something, usually (like in these two examples) something useful or helpful.

Now have a look at sentences 39 and 40:

39 **Shall we pack some sandwiches for lunch?**

40 **Shall we take some flowers to Julia in hospital?**

The question sentence structure "**Shall** we...?" is used to make a suggestion. There are different ways to do this in English. You have already seen how could is used to make suggestions. Using **shall**, as in these sentences, is another very typical way to do it.

Now it's your turn to try and imagine some suitable sentences using **would**, **should** or **shall** for the situations below.

As with the other exercises, there are no fixed answers here, so I have given some possible answers underneath, and some added explanatory notes where appropriate.

It is important that you check your answers with a native speaker to see if the answers you come up with are suitable or not.

1. Make a general comment to your friend that you have no intention of ever going on a cruise as you can't swim and hate the sea. (Sentence 41)

2. Your best friend has just had a big argument with their boyfriend/girlfriend and wants to make up with them. Give them some advice about what to do. (Sentence 42)

3. Tell your friend that yesterday your father told you, "I'll buy you a bicycle for your birthday." (Sentence 43)

4. Tell your husband/wife how your nine-year-old son James refused to give any of his sweets to any of his friends. (Sentence 44)

5. Your friend has to buy a few things from the supermarket but has hurt their back and can't go out. Offer to help them out. (Sentence 45)

6. Tell your younger brother strongly that he is too young to be smoking. (Sentence 46)

7. You are at a party but you don't know your host very well. Politely ask if you can borrow a torch from them as you have to fetch something from your car and it's dark outside. (Sentence 47)

8. Using "I wish", express your desire for your neighbours not to keep leaving their bags of rubbish in the road. (Sentence 48)

9. Express your opinion about increased taxation for high earners. (Sentence 49)

10. Sarah is very annoyed because her dad refused to let her go out last night. (Sentence 50)

SUGGESTED ANSWERS

41 I wouldn't go on a cruise as I can't swim.

42 You should buy your girlfriend a bunch of flowers and send them to her house.

43 My dad said he'd buy me a bicycle for my birthday!

44 He was very naughty, he wouldn't give any sweets away to anybody.

45 Shall I go to the supermarket for you?

THE USES OF WOULD AND SHOULD

46 You should stop smoking, you are too young.

47 Would you be able to lend me a flashlight? I have to get a bottle of wine from the car.

48 I do wish the neighbours wouldn't keep putting their rubbish out on the road! I'm going to have to have a word with them.

49 I don't think people who earn more money should pay a higher percentage of tax.

50 Sarah's dad wouldn't let her go out last night.

TRACK TWELVE

Now listen to Track Twelve on the CD.

In the following paragraph there are six gaps which should be filled using either **would**, **wouldn't**, **should** or **shall**. Read through the paragraph carefully and decide which is suitable for each gap.

My mum asked me if I...(1)...talk to dad about the possibility of going to England together for a holiday, but as soon as I mentioned the word "travel" he shook his head defiantly. He just...(2)...listen to me! He has always said he...(3)...never fly because he's afraid, but we (my mum, my sister and me) have always told him that he...(4)...try to overcome his fear. When I told my mum that he had rejected her suggestion, she winked at me and said, "...(5)...we go without him?" I was surprised by my mother's words as she seemed to be totally serious. I told her that I didn't think it was a good idea. Dad...(6)...be very upset if we did that.

You can hear the completed paragraph on the CD.

TRACK THIRTEEN

Now listen to Track Thirteen on the CD.

SUMMARY

Now you have a chance to look at further example sentences with **would** and **should** expressing the concepts we have considered in this Module.

Here's a breakdown of their major uses:

PERMISSION (WOULD)

Would you mind if I made a quick phone call?

Would your brother mind if I used his hair gel?

FAVOURS (WOULD)

Would you be able to do us a big favour next week? We need someone to feed the cat every evening while we're in Los Angeles.

Would you be able to pay me in cash? That would be a great help.

STATEMENTS OF INTENT (WOULD)

Cat hair makes me sneeze, so I wouldn't get one.

John said he'd move back to the mid-west if he didn't have such a good job here.

There's no way Laura would come to a casino with me – she hates gambling.

You said you'd pay me back last week and you didn't. What's your excuse this time?

REFUSALS (WOULDN'T)

Sorry I'm late. The stupid teacher wouldn't let us leave until we'd finished the test.

Steven wouldn't give us the key to the garage.

WISHES (WOULD)

We're worried about your condition and we wish you'd see a doctor.

I really wish you wouldn't talk about me behind my back.

ADVICE / OBLIGATION (SHOULD)

Your children really should try and arrive at school on time.

We should spend less time talking and more time training.

You should eat more fruit and vegetables.

OPINION / PREDICTION (SHOULD)

There should be more tennis courts at the club; four is not enough for the number of members that there are.

It should be a smooth flight, the weather conditions are very good.

OFFERS / SUGGESTIONS (SHALL)

Shall I give you a hand putting on the spare tyre?

Shall we unpack the cases tomorrow morning? I'm so tired.

TRACK FOURTEEN

Now listen to Track Fourteen on the CD.

THE USES OF MUST AND MIGHT

If you refer back to our concept table for **modal verbs** in the introduction to Part Two, you will see that in this Module we will be talking about obligation (again), deduction, probability and possibility (again).

Let's start with how **must** is used to express obligation, as this concept should be fresh in your mind from what we considered about **should** in the previous Module.

Have a look at sentences 1-10:

1. **You mustn't phone her too late; she usually goes to bed early in the winter.**

2. **I must remember to water the plants before I leave.**

3. **Charlie, you must send in your passport application as soon as possible – it's only a month until we are going!**

4. **You must make sure that you turn all the lights off before leaving.**

5. **We must get the tyres checked on the car before setting off tomorrow.**

6. **I must get to the bank this afternoon to deposit those cheques.**

7. **Mark and Julia, you know how particular Auntie Linda is about manners – you mustn't blow your nose at the dinner table.**

8. **You must stop smoking immediately or you won't have long to live.**

9. **Carl mustn't have any stress over the next few days; he needs to recuperate slowly after the trauma of the accident.**

10. **We must do everything we can to help Joanne during her exams.**

IMPORTANT

1.   **Must** indicates a much stronger **obligation** than **should**. Its use suggests that something is absolutely necessary.

In the last Module you saw how the use of **should** often falls between expressing an obligation and giving advice. Look again at these ten sentences and see how in each one the sense is much stronger than just giving advice. That is evident from each situation.

2.   Four sentences are examples of what can be called 'self-imposed' **obligations**.

In other words the speaker is telling himself/herself something they **must** do (either alone, as in sentences 2 and 6, or with someone else, as in sentences 5 and 10).

3.   The other six sentences express an **obligation** imposed by the speaker on another person/other people, i.e. "You/Someone must do something...".

At this point we need to make a quick mention of **have to**, which is another way that strong obligation is expressed in English. Sometimes **have to** and **must** are interchangeable, but there is an important general difference between them. Look at sentences 11 and 12 and try to see how the use of **have to** differs from the use of **must**:

11   All the children have to sign the register when they arrive at school in the morning.

12   In this country you have to be eighteen before you can start taking driving lessons.

The use of **have to** often relates to regulations imposed from outside. **Must** refers to an obligation that I put on myself or someone puts on me (i.e. it's personal), but **have to** is usually separate from someone's feeling and relates to exterior obligations (impersonal things).

One further very important point. **Must** cannot be used to express the past. In the cases when we need to talk about how an obligation was imposed in the past we have to use **had to**. Have a look at two examples:

13 **My boss said that I had to finish the report by Friday.**

14 **A few months ago I told myself I had to lose weight and get fit.**

It is impossible to use **must** in either of these two sentences because the obligation was imposed in the past.

Most students are familiar with the use of **must** to express obligation, probably because it is usually the first use taught. But there is another vital use of **must** in English – arguably more important than obligation - which students often find difficult to master.

Must is used to make deductions. It reveals assumptions and/or conclusions made by the speaker, based on some information that they have.

Have a look at example sentences 15-17 with the explanatory notes:

15 **Maria must have a lot of stress working at that busy restaurant with her limited English.**

It sounds like Maria is a foreign student working in an English-speaking country. The speaker knows Maria's level of English (it is limited) and imagines how that would cause her stress in her job.

16 **Alan and Hannah hardly ever turn their central heating on. They must be freezing in that house.**

A reasonable assumption to make! Sounds like a frugal couple.

17 **You must be exhausted after the journey – did you stop to eat?**

Clearly the journey has been a long one and the speaker is assuming – again reasonably - that "you" are very tired.

IMPORTANT

In these three sentences, **must** is being used to make an assumption about somebody else. What the speaker is doing in effect is putting himself/herself in the position of the other person and imagining what they themselves would feel like. In sentence 15, for example, the speaker is imagining, "I would have stress if I was in Maria's situation." The same is true for sentences 16 and 17.

However, it is not always true that this use of **must** implies that the speaker is imagining how they themselves would feel in the other person's situation. Have a look at sentence 18:

18 **You must fancy a cup of tea after that walk in the cold, Grandma.**

Here, the speaker is stating what he strongly suspects his Grandmother feels like drinking after her walk. It is not that the speaker is imagining what they themselves would like. The deduction is based on what the speaker knows about Grandma's likes and habits.

▼ **Must** can also be used to imagine a general situation, although without a context to these next three sentences we cannot know if the comments are made generally, or whether they relate to a particular situation and a particular person.

The notes will explain clearly what I mean:

19 **It must be terrible to be married to an alcoholic.**

The context of this could be general – a simple straightforward comment, the truth of which most people can imagine, but not relating to any person in particular that the speaker and his/her listener knows.

Or, the context might be quite different. The listener might be married to an alcoholic and the speaker's comment is designed to offer sympathy. It's also possible that the sentence might be part of a conversation between two people about a third person who finds themself in the situation of being married to an alcoholic.

THE USES OF MUST AND MIGHT

20 **There must be great satisfaction in actually seeing your book published.**

> It's the same thing here. The sentence might be a general comment about the feeling first-time authors surely experience, or it might be a comment made directly to a new author – a comment awaiting confirmation (e.g. "Oh yeah, it's a wonderful feeling"). And again there is a third option – it could be a comment made about a third person.

21 **It must be difficult to adapt to living in another country.**

> I think you get the idea by now. The same possible contexts apply to this situation – it could be general, or it could relate to a particular person who the speaker and listener know.

IMPORTANT

Sentences 19-21 are all *general* comments, because they are expressing things that most people would accept as being true. What the additional notes are pointing out is that a *particular* context might (but equally might not) surround the comment.

> So, **must** can be used as an assumption based on putting ourselves in someone else's position and imagining what they 'must' think/feel like, etc, or it can be used for assumptions/conclusions that we make based purely on *information* or *facts* that we have.
>
> Look at three further examples of this latter sense in sentences 22-24:

22 **Richard goes for a four-mile run every morning before work. He must get up very early.**

The speaker knows Richard's habit of going for a run in the mornings and therefore makes a very logical and almost certain assumption.

23 **My dad must work really hard because I never see him during the week. I'm always asleep by the time he gets home from the office.**

Again, a logical assumption made by the child based on their *knowledge* that dad goes out to work all day and *the fact* that they don't see him in the evenings.

24 **Patrick must smoke a lot; the ashtray on his desk always seems to be full.**

A natural assumption to make.

In these three sentences, the speaker is using certain objective facts to draw a conclusion. Each time the conclusion drawn is almost certain.

▼ **Must** can also be used to draw conclusions which are absolutely certain (i.e. scientifically provable, or beyond reasonable doubt).

Have a look now at sentences 25-27 which are examples of certain deductions, and the notes:

25 **The batteries in the radio are working perfectly, so it must be another problem.**

The radio doesn't work. Someone suggested that the batteries had run out or weren't working, but it has been proved that the batteries do work (probably by trying them in another appliance), so the conclusion is not a theory or a guess. This use of **must** is a certain deduction.

26 **Because we know that oil is not as dense as water, it must rise above it.**

Another certain deduction, scientifically provable.

27 **Only you and I have zippo lighters, and I've got mine here so the one that the cleaner found on the stairs must be yours.**

This sentence is slightly different from the other two in that it cannot be scientifically proved, but it is a conclusion beyond reasonable doubt.

Deductions are often made by removing all other possibilities until we know the truth because there is only one plausible theory left. Read Sherlock Holmes – **must** was one of his favourite words.

▼ **Might** is used to express probability and possibility. Probability is often linked to making deductions, so these two concepts often overlap with each other, as you will see in some of the examples. Have a look at sentences 28-33, with the additional notes, which are examples of **might** expressing probability:

28 **Jim rang to say he might be a bit late because of the road works.**

> This is a deduction that Jim is making based on information that he has. He knows there are road works which are likely to cause a delay to his journey. He is therefore letting somebody know that it is *probable* that he will be late.

29 **You might have a problem trying to persuade the bank manager to give you a loan.**

> We don't have the context here, but the use of **might** tells us that the speaker is basing his opinion on something he knows. Perhaps the person wanting the loan has a low income or a bad credit rating.

30 **Isn't Rachel at home? Try the office – she might be there.**

> The speaker knows Rachel. They guess that the most *probable* place where Rachel is (as soon as it is known she isn't at home) is at the office. This is based on what the speaker knows about Rachel and about her life.

31 **Dad, I might be suspended from school for missing the geography exam.**

> The son/daughter knows that suspension is a *probable* outcome for missing the exam. The comment is based on what is known by the son/daughter about the school rules or normal practice in this kind of situation.

THE USES OF MUST AND MIGHT

32 **We might not have time this morning to pick up those books you ordered.**

Again, there is a degree of deduction here. The speaker is calculating what has to be done this morning and how long it is likely to take. His conclusion is that *probably* collecting the boots will be impossible.

33 **If you're not leaving until 11am, you might not be back before dark.**

This sentence is similar to the last one. Using the facts that he knows (i.e. the length of the journey and the time the sun sets) the speaker is calculating a *probable* outcome. It is quite a reasonable deduction.

IMPORTANT

Probability is not wild guesswork, it is the result of evaluating information.

In each sentence, something more than just a possibility is being expressed. None of the statements are certain, but they are more than just *possible*; they are *probable* or likely. Why? Because they are not guesses, but intelligent opinions based on information and/or facts to which the speaker has access.

Sentences 34 and 35 are examples of how **might** can be used to express just possibility:

34 **I might go to London next year to study English.**

The speaker has clearly not decided yet ('going to' would be used if they had decided) but is entertaining the possibility of going to London next year.

35 **Sean's parents might buy a villa in Florida.**

Again, undecided at the time of speaking. Only a possibility – how many things get talked about and never get done?

THE USES OF MUST AND MIGHT

SEE APPENDIX TWENTY

▼ **Might** can also be used to give a form of advice. In this way it is nearly always used with the verb "to be". Have a look at sentences 36 and 37:

36 **The roads are pretty icy Charles, it might be better to take the train.**

The speaker is advising Charles against driving.

37 **It might be a good idea to phone the company directly – letters can easily be ignored.**

The speaker recommends a more direct and immediate way of approaching the company.

▼ Finally, mention needs to be made of another minor **modal verb**, one which has already come up – back in Module Five. **May**, as well as being used to occasionally ask permission to do something in extremely formal situations, is also used to express possibility and/or probability:

38 **We may be moving house sometime this year.**

39 **I may have to close the shop tomorrow afternoon because of the funeral. I've got no one who can run it for me.**

40 **His parents may be selling the business and emigrating to Australia.**

IMPORTANT

In each of these sentences, **might** could equally be used, without any change of meaning or feeling at all.

Equally, **may** could be used in the other sentences in this Module that use **might**. That might (or may!) seem confusing, and undoubtedly it would be easier for you if I could outline a clear difference between them. But there isn't one.

THE USES OF MUST AND MIGHT

The only thing I can emphasize is that **might** – for whatever reason - is far more commonly used to express probability and possibility than **may**. This is especially true in colloquial English.

Now it's your turn to try and imagine some suitable sentences using **must**, **might** or **have to** for the situations below.

As you are well aware by now, these exercises are designed to make you think about how to fit the **modal verbs** into a context which is given to you. Naturally there are different ways in which different people will think about them, therefore there are no fixed answers. That is why it really is important for you to check your answers with a native speaker if possible.

1. You tell your sister that you are thinking about moving out of home soon to share a flat with your friend Dave. (Sentence 41)

2. You are having to pump up the front-right tyre on your car every morning before leaving for work. What's your conclusion? (Sentence 42)

3. Put an obligation on yourself to finish the book you are reading by the end of this week. (Sentence 43)

4. Explain to your new colleague that the company you are both working for has a policy of not smoking inside the building. (Sentence 44)

5. Arnold has a night job stacking shelves in a local supermarket. Make a comment about this kind of job to your friend. (Sentence 45)

6. Tell your wife that there is a strong possibility that you will have to go to Mexico on business soon. (Sentence 46)

7. Your dad is trying to lose weight by going to the gym every day at lunchtime. Advise him to go first thing in the morning instead. (Sentence 47)

THE USES OF MUST AND MIGHT

8. You are a teacher and have to leave your class for five minutes. Oblige the children in your class not to make any noise while you are gone, so as not to disturb other classes nearby. (Sentence 48)

9. Naomi, a cousin of yours, has just won the national lottery. Make a sentence imagining her feeling. (Sentence 49)

10. Tell your mum that you think it is likely that your wife is pregnant, although it hasn't been confirmed yet. (Sentence 50)

SUGGESTED ANSWERS

41 I might move out soon to go and live with Dave.

42 The tyre must have a puncture.

43 I must finish "A Sense of English" by the end of this week.

44 The company rules are that you have to smoke outside.

45 It must be so boring to do something like that.

46 I might well have to go to Mexico later this month – we've got some potential partners down there.

47 Dad, it might be better to go first thing in the morning and exercise when your stomach is empty.

48 There are other classes at work, so you mustn't make any noise while I'm gone.

49 She must be ecstatic!

50 Mum, we're not sure, but Tanya might be pregnant.

THE USES OF MUST AND MIGHT

THE USES OF MUST AND MIGHT

TRACK FIFTEEN

Now listen to Track Fifteen on the CD.

In the following paragraph there are six gaps which should be filled using either **must**, **might** or **have to**. Read through the paragraph carefully and decide which of them is suitable for each gap.

"Have you heard about Barbara? She...(1)...have to go into hospital again next week."

"Really? No, I hadn't heard. It...(2)...be awful to spend so much time there. We really...(3)...go and visit her."

"I...(4)...not be able to go next week. I...(5)...go on that four-day training course."

"Oh, of course. I'd forgotten about that. Do you think Barbara will get better?"
"I think we have to be prepared for the fact that she...(6)...not get better. She's quite old and very frail."

You can hear the completed paragraph on the CD.

TRACK SIXTEEN

Now listen to Track Sixteen on the CD.

SUMMARY

It's important that you read and think about the sentences in the summary carefully. Seeing and hearing further examples helps to cement your understanding.

Here's a breakdown of the major uses of **must** and **might** (and **have to**):

PERSONAL OBLIGATIONS

I must write to the council about the graffiti in our street.

You must take out comprehensive travel insurance for your round-the-world trip.

My doctor told me I had to stick to the diet religiously for a month and not have any lapses.

IMPERSONAL OBLIGATIONS (HAVE TO)

You have to have a visa to enter China.

It's very simple. To win the game, you have to score more points than anybody else.

ASSUMPTIONS / CONCLUSIONS

You must be delighted to have got the job.

Eric must train very hard – he's not young but he looks in great shape.

You must know how to make a paella after living in Spain for three years.

There must be a bigger bookshop in London than this one.

Being a lawyer must involve a lot of stress.

DEDUCTIONS (MUST)

If the suitcase isn't in the left-side cupboard, it must be in the right-side one.

There's only one key on the ring that I haven't tried, so it must be the one that fits this door.

THE USES OF MUST AND MIGHT

The sun is setting over there, so according to the map, the village we are looking for must be in that direction.

PROBABILITY / POSSIBILITY

Isabel may take up Spanish because of her interest in travelling in South America.

I might be back late tonight, so don't worry about waiting up for me.

The bad news is my flatmates might be leaving. They've found a house they quite like and are considering making an offer for it.

You might have to pay extra for your luggage because it feels overweight to me.

I heard a rumour that your brother might have to quit tennis because of his injury. Is it true?

ADVICE

You might be better off with a girl of your own age!

 TRACK SEVENTEEN

Now listen to Track Seventeen on the CD.

PAST PERFECT MODALS

You have already seen in Module Three how **modal verbs** can be used in a past perfect structure.

The **modal verb** is followed by have and the *past participle* (i.e. **could** *have been*, **must** *have seen*, etc.)

The sense of the **modals** remains the same when used in a past perfect structure as when used in the present.

You have studied the six principal **modal verbs** in Part Two – **can**, **could**, **would**, **should**, **must** and **might**, and brief mentions have been made of **may**, **shall** and **have to**.

In this Module we'll have a look at some example sentences of each of the main **modal verbs** used in a past perfect structure.

IMPORTANT

If you look at the concept table back in the introduction to Part Two, you will see that **can't** (it is always negative) can be used to make deductions.

The rule is simple: **must** cannot be used to make a negative deduction (i.e. **mustn't**). **Mustn't** never expresses the concept of deduction. When you need to make a negative deduction, **can't** is the word you need to use.

Keeping that in mind and taking your time, think carefully about the meaning of sentences 1-4:

1. **After growing up on a farm, it can't have been easy for Giles to adapt to living in a big city.**

2. **Your parents can't have been very happy with your exam results.**

3 **It can't have been Michael you saw in the taxi this morning, Kate. He flew off to the Caribbean yesterday.**

4 **You can't have finished that book already! You only started reading it yesterday.**

How did you get on?

Here's some help.

In the previous Module you saw how **must** is used to make assumptions – sometimes by imagining someone else's situation, and sometimes by drawing a natural conclusion from information that we have. You also saw how **must** is used to make certain 'provable' deductions.

Can't is used in those three ways as well. Hopefully you were able to see that from the examples, but if not, don't worry. Have a look at them again with the added notes:

1 **After growing up on a farm, it can't have been easy for Giles to adapt to living in a big city.**

The speaker imagines Giles 'past' situation, in other words, the past process of adapting to city life. Without a context, we don't know whether Giles still lives in the city or not.

This sentence could equally be expressed by "It must have been difficult for Giles to adapt to living in a big city".

2 **Your parents can't have been very happy with your exam results.**

Melissa didn't get good results, and the speaker assumes – quite naturally – that her parents weren't happy when they found out. Be clear about one thing: the speaker is only assuming at the time of speaking. That means they don't know what the parents' reaction was. They are just drawing a logical conclusion. The next sentence in a context like this one would probably be an admission, something like "No, they weren't happy, you're right." A sentence like this invites a response.

3 It can't have been Michael you saw in the taxi this morning, Kate. He flew off to the Caribbean yesterday.

Kate thought she saw Michael in a taxi this morning, but the speaker knows that Michael went to the Caribbean yesterday. So this is a pretty certain deduction (beyond reasonable doubt, anyway). Kate saw someone she thought was Michael, but almost certainly it was in fact someone else – someone who looked like Michael.

4 You can't have finished that book already! You only started reading it yesterday.

This is a sentence open to interpretation. The speaker could be expressing disbelief, i.e. "I don't believe you", or they could be expressing amazement, i.e. they accept that the reader has finished the book and are marvelling at how quickly they have read it.

The intonation used would almost certainly reveal to a trained ear the speaker's feeling and intention. Listen carefully to this sentence on the CD later on.

Notice how all four sentences are talking about particular situations. Whenever any **modal verb** is used in a past perfect structure, the sentence always relates to a particular situation in the past.

Lastly, **can't** is sometimes used in the present to make deductions. Have a look at sentences 5 and 6 and the notes:

5 Dad, there can't be much further to go now, surely?

A father on a journey somewhere with his son, who sounds fed-up and is hoping that very soon they will be arriving at their destination. He feels like they have been travelling for ages and concludes that they must be nearly there. Again, the sentence invites a response, and would do so even if the son had not tagged "surely?" on to the end of his sentence.

PAST PERFECT MODALS

6 **That new member Paul lost his first round match to Steve Martin. He can't be a very good player!**

> The speaker obviously doesn't think that Steve Martin is a good (tennis) player, and therefore concludes that anyone who loses to him can't be very good either.

 IMPORTANT

In the notes for sentence 1 you saw how an alternative way to express the same deduction is to use **must**. "It can't have been easy" carries exactly the same meaning as "It must have been difficult".

You can do the same thing in each of the other sentences. "Your parents must have been unhappy" (sentence 2), "it must have been someone else you saw" (sentence 3), "we must be nearly there" (sentence 5), etc.

The golden rule again: When used to express deduction, **can't** is the negative of **must**.

Look back quickly at the notes to sentence 6 in Module Two. There you can see one further example of this 'deductive' use of **can't**.

 Now for **could**. Have a look at sentence 7, which is a Third Conditional sentence:

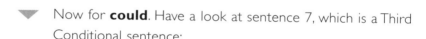

7 **If we had rented a car, we could've gone to some of the more remote areas in the mountains.**

> You will know that this means that the reality was we didn't rent a car. The sentence is expressing a past possibility that *did not happen*.

> The past perfect structure of **could** is often used to express this. Here are some further examples with notes:

8 **I'm silly. I could've called Ruben last week when we were in Barcelona and we could've met up. I just didn't think of it at the time.**

It would have been *possible* to call Ruben to meet up, but I didn't do it.

PAST PERFECT MODALS

9   **We couldn't have bought the house without the financial help of my parents-in-law.**

It would have been too expensive if they hadn't given/lent us some money.

10   **It was a horrific accident. Ashley's injuries could've been much worse than they were.**

Ashley is a lucky man.

IMPORTANT

1.   Sentences 7 and 8 express a kind of *regret*.

The speaker in each of the sentences feels that they didn't do something that would have been good to do. They missed a chance.

2.   Sentences 9 and 10 express the opposite emotion - *relief*.

The speaker in each of these sentences recognizes that the situation could have been much worse than it actually turned out to be.

3.   Back in Module Three we looked at how Third Conditional sentences often express one of these two emotions.

Many of the **modal verbs**, when used in past perfect structures, express *relief* or *regret*. They talk about real situations in the past, and they reveal the feelings and intentions of the speaker.

    A less usual but nevertheless important use of **could** in a past perfect structure is to express *annoyance*. Have a look at sentences 11:

11   **You could've called me, Harry – I was getting worried.**

The speaker was waiting for Harry. He arrived later than expected, and the speaker is expressing their opinion that Harry was naughty not to call them. The intonation will certainly reveal *annoyance*. No other intonation would fit this kind of sentence. The intention of the speaker is to make Harry feel guilty and make him apologize.

103

▼ Finally, have a look at an example of **could** expressing ability in a past perfect structure:

12 **I know that Gareth could've achieved more at school. It's such a shame he was so lazy.**

> Gareth didn't achieve what he should have achieved. He had the ability, but didn't have the right attitude.

IMPORTANT

Have you noticed how the **modal verbs** in past perfect structures are expressing exactly the same concepts that you have already learnt to associate with them throughout Part Two? The only difference is that they are set in the past, and are therefore talking about specific situations that have already taken place.

▼ Let's continue with **would**. You have already seen a lot of sentences in which **would** is used in a past perfect structure (the Third Conditional). Remember that often **would** expresses statements of intent and/or certain results to particular situations (as opposed to mere possibilities). Have a look at sentences 13-17 and the notes:

13 **Even if I had had the money, I wouldn't have gone on the trip to Ecuador.**

> A Third Conditional sentence. The speaker tells us here that a lack of money was not the only reason why he/she did not go on the trip to Ecuador. There is another reason (or reasons) that we don't know without the context. A clear statement of intent about something already past.

14 **Maria's parents would've been shocked by their daughter's behaviour at school.**

> This is in effect half a Third Conditional sentence. "If they had known about it" could easily be added to the beginning or the end of the sentence. But those words do not need to be added as the meaning is already implicit.

15 **I would've slept on the plane but the turbulence was so bad that I couldn't.**

Another clear statement of intent. I wanted to sleep during the flight but it wasn't possible to do so. Remember, the use of **would** makes my intention/decision absolutely clear.

16 **My father would've loved to have visited South Africa before he died.**

The speaker knew his father's wish and clearly states it. A desire that remained unfulfilled.

17 **If Sarah hadn't met you, she would never have developed a passion for painting.**

Another Third Conditional sentence. The speaker declares that Sarah's passion for painting resulted directly from meeting "you" (presumably an artist).

One final sentence with **would**. Sometimes it can be used to offer a kind of retrospective advice:

18 **It would've been better renting an office nearer the city centre, Bobby.**

With hindsight, the speaker reflects that a mistake has been made. Again, *regret* is implied here. Bobby needs his/her office to be nearer the city centre, presumably to boost business.

The main use of **should** in a past perfect structure is clear: to express *regret* about something somebody did (**shouldn't**), or regret at something somebody didn't do (**should**).

Have a look at sentences 19-23:

19 **I shouldn't have got married so young.**

I did get married young, and now I feel that was a mistake.

PAST PERFECT MODALS

20 **You should've brought the washing in last night.**

Probably because it rained, and now the clothes are wet.

21 **We shouldn't have drunk so much last night. We've got a long journey to make today and we're both so tired.**

We probably enjoyed it at the time, but now we are paying the price for the fun of the night before and it doesn't seem worth it.

22 **I should've gone to university when I was eighteen. Studying now is more difficult at my age.**

I am studying now and realize how much more difficult it is later on in life than when one is young.

23 **It's Jules' fault, he shouldn't have told you about the party. It was supposed to be a surprise.**

The speaker is annoyed that Jules has not kept the surprise party a secret and has told someone.

24 **Your brother should've helped you to clean the apartment after the party.**

But he didn't, and it sounds like the other brother had to do it alone.

IMPORTANT

1.   Can you see how **should** continues to carry the sense of *obligation* that we considered back in Module Six?

The only difference is that the *obligation* is in the past, and therefore in each situation it is already too late. That's why *regret* is the result.

Like in sentence 18 (which used **would**), each of these sentences with **should** is offering a form of retrospective advice.

▼ Now have a look at sentences 25-28, in which **might** is used in a past perfect structure to express *probability/possibility*. Read the notes as you go:

25 **Sandra, check your voicemail. Adam might've called us while we were in the meeting.**

It sounds very much like Sandra and her friend are expecting a call from Adam.

26 **We are very lucky to get a room. The hotel might've been fully booked.**

The speaker obviously thought it was *probable* that the hotel would be full. We don't know why, maybe because of the season or because it is a popular hotel.

27 **You took a risk not leaving for JFK until 7.30 Sean, you might've missed your flight!**

The speaker calculates that Sean was lucky not to miss his flight.

28 **I might've seen that film – is it the one in which Morgan Freeman plays a cop?**

The context is obviously a conversation about a film. From what has just been said, I think that I have seen it. The answer to my question will confirm whether the film being discussed is the one I think it is or not.

IMPORTANT

1. Can you see something that sentences 25 and 28 have in common?

In both sentences, we don't know yet whether the *probable* thing happened or not. "Adam might have called..." – we are just about to find out whether he has or not. "I might have seen..." when my question about Morgan Freeman is answered, I will know. The *probable/possible* actions – if they have happened – are in the past, and that's why the past perfect structure is used.

2.   It should be easy now to see what sentences 26 and 27 have in common.

In both, the scenario that the speaker suggests was *probable* didn't actually happen. In other words, we know that the hotel wasn't fully booked and we know that Sean didn't miss his flight.

In sentence 29, consider how **might** is expressing very much a possibility rather than a probability:

(29) **Forget about the exam now, Linda. You might not have done as badly as you think.**

Linda obviously thinks she has done badly in the exam. The speaker is trying to encourage her, but the use of **might** here *does not* suggest he/she thinks it *probable* that Linda has done well. The speaker almost certainly accepts Linda's opinion that she has done badly.

This use of **might** is not a very common one, but you will come across it and you need to recognize it and understand its sense.

The best way to describe this sense is that it imagines the highly *improbable* – quite often in order to try and cheer someone up.

Finally, have a look at sentence 30 which gives us one further use of **might** in a past perfect structure:

(30) **Curtis might've looked OK, but inside I know he's really cut up about the divorce.**

SEE APPENDIX TWENTY ONE

Now for the last of our main **modal verbs**. The use of **must** in past perfect structures never expresses obligation, only

PAST PERFECT MODALS

assumptions/conclusions and certain deductions. Have a look at the six sentences with the notes:

31 **Many investors must've panicked after the financial crash.**

A pretty logical conclusion. A certain deduction.

32 **I can't see Dad's car in the drive; he must've parked out in the road.**

A reasonable assumption, but of course not certain.

33 **Why is your brother so upset? You must've done something to him, Mark.**

The speaker (perhaps a parent) is assuming that the brother being upset is very likely to be connected to something unkind that Mark has done. Perhaps they are playing alone together, or perhaps Mark often upsets his brother.

34 **The prawns I ate last night must've been off because I was very sick during the night and still feel dreadful now.**

A fairly certain deduction.

35 **The car keys aren't here. I must've left them in the office.**

Another fairly certain deduction. It's possible that the keys are somewhere else, but the speaker imagines that by far the most likely place is the office.

36 **The cake's not here, so Ruth must've come and gone.**

A certain deduction. Ruth clearly had an arrangement to pick up the cake from the speaker's house, and has done so while he/she wasn't there.

Being limited to only expressing deductions in the past, **must** is quite easy. Hopefully the sense of this group of sentences is clear for you.

Now it's your turn to try and imagine some suitable sentences using a past perfect modal structure for the following situations. These sentences are more difficult than the other practice exercises you have done in Part Two, because you now have to choose from six possible **modal verbs**. As I always suggest, checking your answers with a native speaker is the only way to be sure that your answers are suitable.

1. You and your friend James had lunch together. You each have identical mobile phones, and as you are walking back to your office James' wife calls you. She doesn't have your number, so what do you deduce has happened? (Sentence 37)

2. Express relief that on a recent trip to Africa you didn't catch malaria, even though you didn't take any tablets with you. (Sentence 38)

3. After your salsa class this evening, you intended to speak to the teacher (Robin) about having some extra help, but he left before you had a chance. (Sentence 39)

4. Express regret that you didn't learn a foreign language when you were young. (Sentence 40)

5. Your younger brother claims he saw a shark in the sea this morning. Because you know he is prone to exaggeration, and also that sharks aren't found in these parts, express to him your disbelief. (Sentence 41)

6. You have just failed your driving test because you felt very nervous. Express your frustration because you believed you had the ability to pass. (Sentence 42)

7. Your friend Mark was supposed to pick you and your wife up from the train station at 6.00, but he hasn't arrived and it's now 6.20. Express a probable/possible reason. (Sentence 43)

8. Your colleague Andy arrives at the office looking hung-over. You know that he went to a party last night, so what do you deduce? (Sentence 44)

9. Your brother usually drives to work in the morning (it takes about five minutes from his house). You go round to his house at midday to put a book that you borrowed from him through his letterbox but you notice that his car is in the drive. You ring the bell to see if he is at home, but he is not. What do you conclude about how he went to work that morning? (Sentence 45)

10. You are really annoyed with your friend who, while using your computer, spilt some coffee over the keyboard but never told you. (Sentence 46)

11. Your sister lost her temper with her boyfriend last night. Express to her that you think it was a mistake. (Sentence 47)

12. A birthday present that your aunt sent you never arrived, and you never knew it had been sent. Explain to her that that is why you never thanked her for it. (Sentence 48)

13. You feel you are lucky because you managed to book a last-minute flight to London in high season. (Sentence 49)

14. Assure your friends that you really wanted to go camping with them last weekend, and the only reason you didn't go was because it was your grandparents' golden wedding. (Sentence 50)

SUGGESTED ANSWERS

37 **We must've taken each other's phone.**

38 **I was lucky. I could've caught malaria.**

39 **I would've spoken to Robin after the lesson, but he left before I had a chance to.**

40 **I should've studied another language when I was young.**

41 **It can't have been a shark you saw. There aren't any around here.**

42 I could've passed the test if I hadn't been so nervous.

43 Mark might've forgotten that he was supposed to pick us up.

44 He must've drunk a lot last night.

45 He must've walked to work, or got a lift with someone.

46 You could've told me! Did you think I wouldn't notice?

47 You shouldn't have lost your temper last night.

48 I'm so sorry. Of course I would've written to thank you if I'd known about your kind gesture.

49 There might not have been any available seats at this time of year. I was definitely lucky to find a flight.

50 I would've gone with you if it hadn't been for my grandparents' golden wedding.

TRACK EIGHTEEN

Now listen to Track Eighteen on the CD.

In the following paragraph there are six gaps which should be filled using a **modal verb**. The past perfect structure is already in place for you. Read through the paragraph carefully and decide which of them is suitable for each gap.

"You...(1)...'ve told me about your proposed trip to Mexico. I think it's really mean of you that you didn't."

"I...(2)...'ve told you, but we wanted to keep it a surprise until the plans were finalized. Anyway, you know now, and you're very welcome to come if you want to."

"I don't know. How much is it going to cost?"

"If we'd bought the tickets last month, it...(3)...only have cost $800, but now the same all-inclusive deal is offered for $1000."

"So, you...(4)...'ve bought the tickets before! I don't want to pay $1000."

"That price does include everything though. The only extra money you need is for what you will personally spend."

"Who else is coming?"

"Sandra and Isabel are definitely coming, Christian is a maybe and Cliff said he...(5)...'ve come but he can't get the time off work. Oh, and Rachel is supposed to be coming by this morning to tell us whether she's coming or not."

"Look, there's a note from her on the table. She...(6)...'ve been here already."

You can hear the completed paragraph on the CD.

 TRACK NINETEEN

Now listen to Track Nineteen on the CD.

SUMMARY

Have a look here at some further example sentences.

NEGATIVE DEDUCTIONS

It can't have been a fox; there aren't any around here. It must've been a cat.

Simon's lying. He can't have read the letter because he didn't know anything about the party.

POSSIBILITY (COULD)

You could've started a fire here, playing with those matches! I'm very disappointed in you!

RELIEF (COULD)

That golf ball could've landed on your head! Thank goodness it didn't.

REGRET (COULD)

I could've become a professional basketball player if I hadn't spent so much time partying when I was in my teens.

ANNOYANCE

You could've stopped to give me a lift – it was starting to rain.

ABILITY

I'm proud of the players, they couldn't have tried any harder. We're gallant losers today.

INTENTION

Uncle Robert always said he would've liked to learn how to ski.

I wouldn't have paid the fine. I would've argued my case with the traffic warden until he agreed with me!

CERTAIN RESULT

My mum wouldn't have married my dad if he hadn't had a good job at the time.

ADVICE

It would've been wiser to have kept quiet and not said anything.

REGRET (SHOULD)

You shouldn't have cooked so late last night, it made too much noise for the other residents.

I should've asked Lisa to marry me before I went off on the trip.

PROBABILITY

Check the drawer in your desk. You might've put your purse in there.

I might've spent all my money if you hadn't been with me.

ASSUMPTIONS / CONCLUSIONS

Did you only get back yesterday? You must've been exhausted last night.

Your mum must've been furious when she saw the state of the house. She probably promised herself never to go away again!

DEDUCTIONS (MUST)

It's very warm in here. Jason must've forgotten to switch the central heating off.

James must've picked up the letter by mistake with the rest of his mail.

TRACK TWENTY

Now listen to Track Twenty on the CD.

CD TRANSCRIPTS

- What time are you back tomorrow?
- Well, I'm taking the 4.30 flight from Chicago, so we should arrive around 7.00.
- OK, **if I leave the office on time, I'll pick you up from the airport**. Call me as soon as you've landed.

- Any jobs you want me to do while you're gone?
- Yes, there is something. **If we're not back by 5.00 put the chicken in the oven**. It's on the counter all ready. You just need to preheat the oven for about fifteen minutes. But we should be back before then anyway.
- OK, well I'll keep an eye on the time.

- I've never been much of a coffee drinker anyway. I've always preferred tea.
- Well, my husband and I drink both, but Bill's got a problem at the moment. **If he drinks coffee after 9.00, he can't sleep**. So he's trying to get used to drinking a cup of tea after dinner instead of coffee.

- Did I tell you Marie and I are planning a trek around South America next summer?
- No, you didn't. Hey Don, **if you go to Argentina, you must try the popular soup called "Guisos"**. I tried it when I was there and it's delicious.

- Did you know I've still got some holiday to take this year? And I have to take it before Christmas – it won't carry over.
- Well I'm off from Monday, so **if you take next week off, we could have a few days away together**. What do you think?
- That sounds like heaven. I'll talk to my boss tomorrow.

- My parents are seriously thinking about selling that apartment in Manhattan they bought.
- That was two or three years ago, wasn't it?
- Four now. They bought it as an investment.
- Four! Well, the property must have doubled in value in that time. I mean, **your parents could buy a villa in Florida if they sell the apartment in Manhattan**.
- They could, but they won't. They want to buy something in Mexico.

- What's the news on my car?
- You're definitely going to need a new fuel pump. And there are one or two other minor things.
- Look, I've got a proposal for you. **If you fix my car for free, I'll give your son ten hours of free math tutoring**. How does that sound?
- Um, I think we should keep things separate. I'll pay you for your teaching and you pay me for the labour.

- Our son John has got his driving test next week. His father's been telling all our friends, **"If my son passes his driving test, I'm going to buy him a car."** John doesn't know that of course, and I don't think it's particularly wise to be telling everyone just yet. I hope he doesn't find out, at least not before he takes the test.
- Well, I hope he passes.

- Richard, I think the boys should help me more with the housework. They spend too much time surfing the net.
- Yeah, you're right. I'll make a deal with them. Hey boys! **You guys can play on the computer until supper if you promise to wash up**.
- You should make them do the work first and then let them play.
- Don't worry, I've made them promise and I'll make sure they keep it.

- Did you say you were going to call uncle Sam tonight?
- Well I was going to, but I'm really engrossed in this TV programme about how to cook the perfect steak. It might be too late to call by the time it's over.
- Well, **if you call him, thank him again for the birthday present**. Tell him I'm going to wear it this weekend for Isabel's wedding.

- Do you know if Sarah is going to be at the party?
- Sarah Macefield? I don't know.
- **Could you tell her to call me if you see her?**
- Sure. If she's there I'll tell her.

- The statistics tell the story really. In 1995 just under 90% of Brazilians were living in cities. And this is the fifth largest country in the world, both in terms of population and size. People are literally flocking to cities like Sao Paolo to try and improve their lives. And yet the reality is that **if urban migration continues to increase at the current rate, there'll be an even bigger poverty problem in a few years**. Cities are overcrowded and their resources are overstretched.

- Michelle, as your teacher my assessment of you is clear. There's no doubt in my mind that **you should pass the exam if you study hard**. It depends on you. What you mustn't do is think that you can just cruise through — you are going to have to put in the study time.

- Jason, I really think you should go and see the doctor. You seem to me to be a bit worse than last night.
- I really don't want to take any antibiotics. I'd like to fight this thing off myself.
- Well, **if you refuse to call the doctor, you should at least take some aspirin**.
- OK. Can you bring me some with another glass of orange juice?

- Sorry to trouble you miss, I need another three dollars to buy my train fare home. Could you help me out? I wouldn't ask if I wasn't desperate.
- Look, I'm not giving you money to go and have another drink at my expense. I can smell the alcohol on your breath. And I'll tell you now very clearly, that **if you come to my house asking for money again I'll call the police**.

- Martin, I know you don't want to leave your hometown, but **you'd definitely have more chance of getting a job if you looked in the city**.
- I know I would. But the problem is my mother. She's not well, Louise. I need to find a job locally to be able to stay near her.

- I don't think Sylvia is ever going to forget Robert. She told me yesterday that **if she ever saw him again, she'd cry with joy.**
- Well, for her sake I hope she can forget him. I don't think he's ever going to come back here.

- I worked in non-fiction publishing for a number of years, so I like to think that my opinion carries some weight. I think that **if a leading publisher saw your work, they might want to publish it**. I think it's worth approaching some of them.
- Do you really think so?
- Well, you've nothing to lose.

- **If Susan lived in France for a few months, she could really perfect her French.** At the moment she has a good private teacher who is from Nice, and she studies with him once a week. She's reached a very high level now and is really at the point where it's difficult to get any better without actually going to live in the country for a year or two.

- I started eating hot food when I visited China the Christmas before last because the weather was so cold.
- That's interesting, because you never used to like spicy food, did you?
- No, I didn't. But since then I've become addicted. I've even started adding chilli powder to lots of plain dishes.
- **You could eat spicy food as often as you wanted if you lived in Korea.** Did you know a lot of their food is extremely spicy?
- No I didn't. I've never tried Korean food.

- My parents business is still going very well, and they're not thinking about giving up just yet. My dad would be bored without the work.
- But, they could retire and go and live somewhere in the sun if they sold their business now.
- Well, when they feel ready I'm sure that's what they'll do.

- John and Andrea didn't look happy last night. Do you know what's going on?
- John told me at the office yesterday that Andrea wants to move to a smaller apartment because their mortgage repayments are so high and they're really struggling. But John doesn't want to give up the house and would rather take another job in the evenings to earn the extra money. He's not going to change his mind.
- I don't think that's right, I think he putting his family under a lot of pressure. **If he wasn't so stubborn, he'd accept Andrea's suggestion**.
- Well, maybe finally he'll have to.

- Tim, did you see that very interesting report on Third World debt last night?
- No I didn't. My lifestyle's changing Pete, and it's all because of my new job. **I'd watch the late night politics programme every day if I didn't have to get up early for work in the morning**, but my alarm goes off at 4.45 these days. I go to bed about 10.00!

- Even though the traffic is terrible, I have to say that **if I had a car, I would drive to work,** and the reason is that I could then listen to the radio on the way.
- Well, I have a car, and I don't drive to work as you know. I used to, but the stress from the traffic makes you feel tired before you even get to the office.

- So, the holiday wasn't good?
- Oh, it was a disaster. Everything was wrong. The food was awful, there were cockroaches in the bathroom, the water was only hot at certain times during the day – I mean, a holiday from hell basically. **We wouldn't go back to that hotel (even) if you paid us!**
- It sounds like you're due some compensation.

- Charlotte has told me that she spends about four hours every evening using the computer. I don't want to do any tests on your daughter at the moment, Mr Roberts, because I think the problem may have a simple solution in a change of lifestyle. I believe that **if she used the computer less, she wouldn't get so many headaches**.
- What do you suggest, doctor?
- Try limiting her to an hour a day and let's see if the headaches stop.

- I miss you so much. I think about you all the time. I can't bear being so far away from you. **I'd fly to where you are right now if I had wings**. I'm always dreaming of the next time I'm going to see you.

- Imagine you could move in time to any period, past or present, and any place? Where would you go?
- Hmm. I'd go back to the time that Columbus discovered America and be on one of his ships. Can you imagine the moment when they first sighted land?
- Yeah.
- What about you?
- **If we could travel in time, I'd go back to the 1960s** in London, and be a part of Beatlemania and watch England win the World Cup in 1966.

- I think you're very lucky. I'd love to have a sibling.
- Well, believe me, **if you had three sisters, you'd understand my stress**. Mine have been vying with each other their wholes lives – and it hasn't changed even now, in spite of the fact that they're all over twenty.

- I have a real dilemma Todd. I had a letter from a developer the other day offering me a very large sum of money for my house. I hadn't been thinking about selling at all. The letter was totally unexpected. **If you were me, what would you do?**
- Well, surely it depends on the amount you've been offered. You probably need some professional advice and a valuation done of your house and land. You might even be able to ask for a higher price.

- What do you think would be the best way to approach Mr Turner about the problem? Shall I call him?
- **If I were you, I'd write a letter to him first and wait for his response**. If you meet him or talk to him on the phone, you might end up losing your temper and saying something you regret later.

- The thing is Michelle, you've given a lot to the company over the years, and I think they really need you. **So I'd ask your boss for a pay rise if I were you**.
- But I don't want to create any uncomfortable atmosphere.
- You're too soft Michelle. You deserve better and you need to be assertive with them. Not aggressive, but assertive.

- Have you heard Gary's news? His company's sending him to Rome for three years.
- Really? How does he feel about it?
- I think he's a bit apprehensive. It'll be a big change.
- **I'd study Italian, if I were him – it'll be difficult living in Rome without being able to speak the language**.
- Yes, I think he's going to.

TRACK SIX

- I didn't think the film was that good, but I did see it on my own, maybe that was a mistake.
- **If you'd seen it with us, you'd have enjoyed it more**. You know what we're like when we get together.

- My uncle and aunt have just come back from a disastrous package holiday in the Caribbean. **They would've complained very strongly if the company hadn't offered them a free cruise as compensation**.

- Actually we didn't go in the sea at all. It was very crowded and we just didn't feel like it.
- Really? **I would've swum in the sea every day if I'd been with you last week in Hawaii**.

- Jimmy, your friends look bored. I'm afraid that maybe they felt obliged to accept my invitation to come here.
- No, no. **They wouldn't have come if they hadn't wanted to**. Don't worry about them at all.

- I think you should have talked to Isabel a long time ago about all this.
- **If I'd known she was upset, I would've talked to her**. Jack, I honestly had no idea how she felt.

- It was disappointing. It should have been a really close fight, but the injury spoilt it.
- Yeah, absolutely. **Tyson could've won if he'd been fully fit**.
- Hopefully they'll have a rematch next year.

- Kelly, you turned up at just the right time. I was getting mad at him.
- Yeah, that was pretty obvious!
- **If you hadn't come at that moment, I might've lost my temper completely.** Who knows what I might've done to him?

- **John might not have forgiven his wife if he'd known that it wasn't her first affair.**
- What? She's done it before?
- Yes.
- And he doesn't know?
- No. He's forgiven her because he thinks it's a one time affair.

- You know how controlling Naomi's parents are. They don't want her to work until she's graduated.
- I know. Do you remember about a year ago she wanted to apply for that part time modelling position that was advertised? **She could've gotten that job if her father had let her go to the interview.**
- Oh yes. And it would've helped pay for her studies.

- Alistair, you're mad. **If you hadn't been so rude to your boss, you might've got promotion.**
- Well, I don't regret anything. I had to say what I said to him.

- I've been doing the same job now for over twenty years, and I don't have any prospects of ever doing anything else. **My life could've been so different if I'd studied hard at school.** I could've gone to university and given myself a much better chance. In hindsight I deeply regret my laziness.

- **If I'd known that Maria wasn't going to the party, I wouldn't have gone either.**
- Oh, come on! You had a good time.
- No I didn't. I only went because I wanted to see her. I'm in love with her.

- It's good to see you both again. How was Japan?
- It was great; the only thing I'd say is that **if we'd learnt Japanese, we'd have had a much richer experience living in Tokyo.** We should've made more effort.

- How are Simon and Brian this morning?
- John, I'm not happy with you. **Simon and Brian wouldn't have been so ill during the night if they hadn't drunk so much at the restaurant.** You're their father! How can you encourage them to drink like that?

- Stephanie, **if you'd waited to sell your house, you could've gotten a lot more for it.**
- I know that, but I sold at that time because my son had a serious health problem and we needed money quickly for an operation.

- I'm so happy that you're now a non-smoker. **If you hadn't seen that documentary on the dangers of smoking, you'd never have quit,** would you?
- No, I think seeing that program was the prompting that I needed.

- Thanks Sally. **I would've eaten that if you hadn't told me there was meat in it!** And my stomach would've had a hard time because I haven't eaten meat for years!

- Anne, thank you so much for telling us about the London Philharmonic Orchestra being in town. **We wouldn't have gone to the concert if you hadn't recommended it.**
- It was my pleasure. I knew you'd enjoy it.

- I was under a lot of pressure, **my parents would've grounded me if I hadn't passed the exam.**
- You did really well anyway.

- Sarah's really happy with Will. I'm so glad that things have worked out for her.
- Yes. **She would've been miserable if she had married Kevin.** Will's definitely the right one for her.
- I think so.

TRACK EIGHT

- Well, it's a fact of science. **If you heat water to 100 degrees centigrade, it boils.**

- Neither my husband or I are morning people. **If we don't have to get up early, we usually read the newspaper in bed with a cup of coffee.**

- Do you think your parents would be interested in this? A gastronomic holiday in the south of France, sampling wines and classical French cooking.
- **My parents aren't adventurous. If they go abroad, they never try any local food.** My father would be fine with the wine though!

- Lucy, you've done very well, but don't forget that your father really made everything possible. **If he hadn't invested in your business from the outset, you wouldn't have a beautiful four-bedroom detached house in the suburbs of Los Angeles to live in.**
- I know that. I owe a lot to my father.

- **I'd play football every week if I hadn't injured my knee last year. Now I only play twice a month.**
- Surely you shouldn't play at all?
- Well, the osteopath said I could, but just not every week.

- **If they were sensible, James and Tracey would never have paid so much for a one-bedroom flat.** They didn't research the market well enough.
- Well, we all make mistakes. It is the first property they've bought.

- Recently you've been very distant from me. It makes me doubt that you really love me.
- Come on, think about it. **If I didn't love you Nikki, I wouldn't have moved to Colorado to be with you.** I'm just stressed out at the moment by my mother's situation.

- Right, what's your plan for the day?
- Well, **if you're using the computer this afternoon, I'll clean the office and go to the bank and the post office** then. And I'll write my letters this morning.

- Jonathan wants to use his savings to open his own restaurant.
- Well, it's a risk, but at the same time he's lucky. **If I were setting up a business, I'd have to take out a bank start-up loan.** I don't have any capital.

- We weren't at home. I think we've been very lucky.
- Well, **if the dogs hadn't been barking, I'm sure the burglars would've come to our house instead of next door.**
- Yes, you're probably right.

- **This morning we would've gone for a walk if it hadn't been raining.** It's very frustrating, the dogs need a good run.

- Please be careful Alex. I really don't think you should go.
- I have to go Monica. Now listen, **if I haven't phoned you by midnight, call the police and tell them where I am.**
- Don't go, Alex…please.

- I'm very serious about this. There are no more excuses. **If you haven't finished your homework by the time I get home, I'll call your teacher and ask him to put you in detention.** That's a promise.

- What happens if no one comes forward with the winning ticket?
- **If nobody claims the car, it will be sold and the money given to charity.** Just like with the National Lottery.

- I've heard a rumour that **if the staff aren't given a pay rise, they're going to strike.**
- Really? That'll set the cat among the pigeons!

- I was just so nervous at the thought of making that phone call. My mouth was all dry and my tongue just froze. I needed help, Jim, surely you can understand that?
- **If it'd been me, I wouldn't have asked Matthew to help me.** I think it's something that you needed to do on your own. You've got to overcome your fears.

- I think you rushed your decision a bit. **If I'd been you, I would've asked for more time to think about it.** It's such a big decision to get married.
- I know it seems like that, but I have been expecting his proposal, so I have thought it through.

- Simon came off straight away when he took the knock. You could see it in his face that his game was over.
- **If it'd been Felix, he would've played on in spite of the injury.**
- Yeah, Felix is extremely tough. It would take something very serious to get him off the pitch.

- I saw this guy slip his hand into the old lady's bag and pinch her wallet. I immediately shouted out to attract everyone's attention, and as he started running, I threw a tin of tuna at him that I had in my shopping bag. I mean, **what would you have done if you'd been me?**

- I'd probably have done exactly the same. Did you hit him?
- No, the tuna missed and hit a bench.

- Mr Warren?
- Yes.
- **If you'd like to take a seat in the waiting room, I'll be with you shortly**.

- We had a lot of free time, so I decided to use it by learning the languages of the places where I was based. **I could speak English, Spanish and Italian fluently by the time I left the army**.

- It's strange, **Susan's brother couldn't ride a bicycle until he was eighteen**. He had his driving licence before he could cycle!

- Peter, **can you fix my computer for me**? I think it has a virus or something. It's very slow.
- I'll have a look at it later on today.

- **It can be very embarrassing when you are talking to someone you've met before and you can't remember their name**.
- Oh yes! That happened to me last week at the parents' meeting at school. The mother of one of Joe's friends. In the end I had to apologize and ask her her name again.

- Why isn't Andrew here yet?
- David, **we couldn't get through to him for half-an-hour because his phone was switched off during the concert**.
- Well, let's keep calling him!
- No, he's on his way now. He's coming directly from the concert hall.

- Hi Bob, it's good to see you! Where's Ruby?
- **Ruby couldn't come unfortunately Barbara; she isn't well**.
- Oh, I'm so sorry to hear that. Give her my love. I'll stop by to see her some time next week.

- Hello?
- Brad, it's me. Look, **can I come over to watch the game with you tonight?** Joe's got some of her friends coming round.
- Sure, man. Come and help Andre and I drink a fridge full of Budweiser.

- Have you had a fun summer Chuck?
- Yeah, dream on. **I couldn't go out at all during the holidays - my parents made me study all day**.
- Heh, that's too bad.

- How about Martin and Victoria?
- **You can bring the kids to the reception as long as they behave themselves**. It is a formal occasion, so keep a good eye on them, especially during the speeches.

- Lysa, I really need your help.
- What do you need?
- **Could I borrow your car for about three hours tomorrow afternoon? I've got to pick up some boxes from the warehouse.**
- Of course you can.

- **Rich, could you give me a hand clearing out the attic sometime? I think a lot of the stuff up there is yours**.
- OK. I'm free tomorrow afternoon. What about doing it then?
- For me, the sooner the better.

- Terry, **can I ask you a favour? Can you answer the phone if it rings in the next few minutes; I've got to go to the bank**.
- OK, but what do I say?
- Just take a message and a phone number and tell whoever it is that I'll call them back shortly.

- How long are you going to be away?
- Only for two weeks.
- **I could lend you my rucksack for your trip if you want**.
- Could you? That'd be such a help. Thanks man.

- I'm really not in the mood to study right now.
- Nor am I. **We could go to the beach now for an hour while the sun's shining and study later on this afternoon**.
- We're lazy aren't we?
- Yes!
- Let's go.

- Michelle's still really upset about us missing out on that new house. She blames me for not having put the offer in sooner.
- You need to do something. **You could take her away for a romantic weekend somewhere and try and patch things up**. What do you think?
- Yeah, maybe something like that would be good.

TRACK FOURTEEN

- Mr Baker, you look worried. What's the matter?
- **Would you mind if I made a quick phone call?** It's rather urgent. I've left my mobile at home.
- Yes, of course. Use the phone in my office. You'll have more privacy.

- Susan, I've run out of hair gel. **Would your brother mind if I used some of his?**
- Go ahead and use it. He won't even know.

- Mary, **would you be able to do us a big favour next week?** We need someone to feed the cat every evening while we're in Los Angeles.
- Oh, unfortunately I'm not going to be here next week either. I'm going up to Oregon on business. I would've been happy to help.

- Well, thanks for the class. I'll get my chequebook.
- Ray, could I ask you a favour? **Would you be able to pay me in cash this week? That would be a great help**.
- I think that should be OK. Let me go and see what's in my wallet.
- Thank you Ray.

- Lee and Steffanie have now decided to keep that stray cat that wandered into their house last week. So, they now have six cats – together of course with their two dogs and the horse.
- **Cat hair makes me sneeze, so I wouldn't get one**, never mind six!

- I know for a fact that John misses a lot of things from his past. He said to me **he'd move back to the mid-west if he didn't have such a good job here**.
- Well, his parents are there for a start, aren't they?
- Yes, and all his old friends from school.

- If your mum's going to baby-sit on Saturday, why don't you get Laura to come with us?
- **There's no way Laura would come to a casino with me – she hates gambling**.
- Tell her that beginners usually win.
- That won't make any difference.

- Mike, **you said you'd pay me back last week and you didn't. What's your excuse this time?**
- I had to change a tyre on my car unexpectedly. I'm really, really sorry. This time next week you'll have your money – you have my word.

- Hello, where have you been?
- **Sorry I'm late. The stupid teacher wouldn't let us leave until we'd finished the test**.
- Better late than never I suppose. Right, let's get started.

- **Steven wouldn't give us the key to the garage**, Will. He said there's some valuable stuff in there and for security reasons he'd have to ask you first.
- OK. I'll give him a call.

- Jane, **we're worried about your condition and we wish you'd see a doctor**.
- You know how much I hate doctors and conventional medicine. Give me another couple of days using this natural stuff and let's see how I am at the end of the week.

- Sarah, I've not happy about what you did at all. **I really wish you wouldn't talk about me behind my back**. If you think I'm in the wrong, come and tell me to my face next time.

- Mr Harris, **your children really should try and arrive at school on time**. They've been consistently late for the last two weeks.
- Look, it's great to discuss these ideas and plans, etc, but **we should spend less time talking and more time training**.

- If you're serious about losing weight, you'll have to change your diet. Less chocolate and red meat. And **you should eat more fruit and vegetables**.

- We came here on Saturday and couldn't get a game for about an hour. We just sat and drank tea in the Clubhouse.
- Yeah. **There should be more tennis courts at the club; four is not enough for the number of members that there are**.

- I am a little nervous. It's my first time to fly.
- Really? Well, **it should be a smooth flight, the weather conditions are very good**. Try and enjoy it.

- You look like you're having trouble. **Shall I give you a hand putting on the spare tyre?**
- Thank you. Some help would be great.

- **Shall we unpack the cases tomorrow morning? I'm so tired.**
- Yes, let's have a nightcap and then hit the sack.

TRACK SEVENTEEN

- **I must write to the council about the graffiti in our street**. It's a worsening problem and it's devaluing property.

- Lisa, **you must take out comprehensive travel insurance for your round-the-world trip**. You'll be visiting a lot of countries. Don't go without full insurance.
- Don't worry; I'm going to sort that out on Monday.

- How's that weight program you're on going, Elena?
- **My doctor told me I had to stick to the diet religiously for a month and not have any lapses**. But I'm finding it really difficult!

- What's your nationality sir?
- British.
- **You have to have a visa to enter China**.
- How long will it take to process one?
- Five days, sir.

- It looks like such a complicated game.
- It is, but the objective? **It's very simple. To win the game, you have to score more points than anybody else**.

- I know you've wanted a change of direction in your professional life for some time. **You must be delighted to have gotten the job**.
- Yes I am. I'm very ready for a fresh challenge.

- **Eric must train very hard – he's not young but he looks in great shape**.
- Well, he goes to the sports club every day except Sunday and plays tennis, does a half-an-hour workout in the gym and has a swim.

- Let's get Andrew to make us a paella for lunch tomorrow. **You must know how to make a paella after living in Spain for three years**, don't you Andrew?
- Actually I don't. I enjoyed eating paella many times, but I never cooked it myself – and I wouldn't know where to start. So count me out of that one!

- I can't find what I'm looking for. **There must be a bigger bookshop here in London than this one**, isn't there?
- Yes, there is. Let's go to Foyles near Charing Cross, and I'm sure they'll have what you want.

- My wife often works until well past midnight. And she's always out of the house by 8.00 in the morning.
- **Being a lawyer must involve a lot of stress**.
- Yes of course, but she loves it. And she's very good at what she does.

- John! The suitcase isn't here!
- Well, **if it isn't in the left-side cupboard, it must be in the right-side one**. I know it's not anywhere else in the house because I've checked.

- Have you still not managed to open that door?
- There're a lot of keys on this ring! **There's only one that I haven't tried, so it must be the one that fits this door**.
- Well hurry up and open it.

- Are we lost?
- No, I think we're OK. **The sun is setting over there, so according to the map, the village we are looking for must be in that direction**.
- Are you sure?
- Yes. Come on, let's go.

- I was talking to Isabel yesterday. **She may take up Spanish because of her interest in travelling in South America**.
- Give her Carlos' number. He teaches private lessons.
- I mentioned Carlos, but Isabel said she wants to study in a group.

- Shall we eat when you get back?
- No, **I might be back late tonight, so don't worry about waiting up for me**. I've got to clean Andrew's computer for him and I think it'll take a while.

- How's your new accommodation?
- Well, **the bad news is my roommates might be leaving. They've found a house they quite like and are considering making an offer on it**. I've only been living there three weeks. I can't pay the rent on my own and need to find some new tenants quickly.

- We need to go now, I have to check in before 9.00.
- Tess, **you might have to pay extra for your luggage because it feels overweight to me**. Do you want to take anything out?
- No, it's too late now. I have money on me if I have to pay extra.

- Sarah, **I heard a rumour that your brother might have to quit tennis because of his injury. Is it true?**
- He's waiting for the result of a scan on his knee, and then we'll know more.

- How's it going with Charlotte?
- Oh, sometimes it feels like I'm more of a father to her than a boyfriend. She gets upset about the smallest of things.
- **You might be better off with a girl of your own age!** I told you that before you got involved with her.

TRACK TWENTY

- Last night I saw what looked like a fox in your garden. Is that possible?
- No. **It can't have been a fox; there aren't any around here. It must've been a cat**.

- When did you send the letter?
- Last Thursday. Simon told me he got it on Saturday and that he read it immediately.
- Well, I'm sorry but **Simon's lying. He can't have read the letter because he didn't know anything about the party**.

- How many times have I had to tell you about the dangers. **You could've started a fire here, playing with those matches! I'm very disappointed in you!**

- Wooaah! Someone needs some lessons! **That golf ball could've landed on your head! Thank goodness it didn't**.
- We're a good twenty yards off the fairway and that missed me by a couple of inches!

- Did you ever consider a career in sport?
- Not seriously, although my uncle always said that **I could've become a professional basketball player if I hadn't spent so much time partying when I was in my teens**. But I don't know about that, and I certainly don't regret anything.

- Hi! You look drenched.
- Mike, I can't believe you. **You could've stopped to give me a lift – it was starting to rain** when you passed.
- I was in a hurry to get to the bank before it closed. And I didn't think it was going to suddenly pour down as it did. Sorry!

- It's obviously devastating to have lost such a big game – where did things go wrong today in your opinion?
- I just think we were beaten by a better team. **I'm proud of the players, they couldn't have tried any harder. We're gallant losers today**. I just give credit to the opposition.

- I think the important thing is not to have any regrets. If you want to do something, go for it!
- **Uncle Robert always said he would've liked to learn how to ski**.
- There's an example. He never learned and he missed out.

- You won't believe what happened to me this morning. I double parked for two minutes to help an old woman pick up some fruit that had fallen out of her shopping bag, and while I was doing that the traffic cop wrote me out a ticket.
- Did you explain it to him?
- Yes, of course. But it didn't make any difference. I ended up paying the fine on the spot.
- **I wouldn't have paid the fine. I would've argued my case with the cop until he agreed with me!**

- People were more practical in the old days. It wasn't just about being in love with someone.
- Yes it's true. Take my parents for example. **My mum wouldn't have married my dad if he hadn't had a good job at the time**.

- Do you think I did the right thing in telling David what really happened?
- In my opinion **it would've been wiser to have kept quiet and not said anything**.

- Anthony, **you shouldn't have cooked so late last night, it made too much noise for the other residents**.
- Oh come on! It wasn't that late.
- Well, I saw Adam and Sandra this morning and they asked where you were. They want to have a word.

- **I should've asked Lisa to marry me before I went off on the trip**. If we'd made the commitment to each other then I don't think we'd have broken up.
- It's easy to say that with hindsight, Ivan. Don't be too hard on yourself.

- Dave, I can't find my purse. Have you seen it?
- **Check the drawer in your desk. You might've put it in there**.
- I've already looked there. Oh! Here it is – in my inside jacket pocket.

- You lost a lot of money last night playing Blackjack.
- Well, it could've been worse. **I might've spent all my money if you hadn't been with me**. Thanks for stopping me.

- Hi Charlie! Did you have a good trip?
- Great. We got back yesterday afternoon.
- **Did you only get back yesterday? You must've been exhausted last night**.
- Yeah, better now though. We've had a long sleep.

- I slept late this morning and didn't have time to clean up after the party.
- Really? **Your mum must've been furious when she saw the state of the house. She probably promised herself never to go away again!**

- Jason said he was going out at about 6.00, which was four hours ago.
- **It's very warm in here. He must've forgotten to switch the central heating off**.
- Well, he's very naughty then.

- I can't find the letter from the real estate agency. It was here this morning with the other mail.
- **James must have picked it up by mistake with the rest of his mail**. All the letters were together in one pile.
- Let's call him and see.

APPENDICES

APPENDIX ONE

The **First Conditional** can also be used to give advice, as in sentence 6. Here an action (practising regularly) and a result (quick improvement) are expressed, but the intention of the speaker is to encourage a certain course of action, i.e. to practise every day. The sentence offers advice.

In sentence 8, the advice is strong and indirect because it focuses on the negative result of not doing something, rather than the benefits of doing the right thing. Rather than advice, this kind of sentence can be interpreted as a warning. Another use of the **First Conditional** is to warn or threaten.

APPENDIX TWO

Only three of these sentences express threats, two strong and one mild. The others express varying degrees of advice, and two of those (asterisked) express personal opinion and include only implicit advice.

I hope you can see clearly which sentences fall into which category.

Four of these sentences follow the classic structure (numbers 13, 15, 18 and 20). In five of them (numbers 12, 14, 16, 17 and 19) the use of a modal verb replaces the use of **will**. In the other one (number 11) the imperative - an order - is used.

APPENDIX THREE

Imagine the situation. John has just been invited by his friend to go out for a drink. John is at the office and still has a lot of work to do, and doesn't know if he will be able to finish or not. In one of the two responses, the speaker (John) has already made up his mind. In the other, he has refused to commit himself to going out for a drink.

It should be clear now, if it wasn't before, that in sentence 26 John is leaving his options open. *He doesn't want to decide now*, because he doesn't know how he will feel after finishing work. Maybe he will be too tired to go out for a drink and will want to go home. So, the important point is that going out for a drink or not *will depend on his feeling*.

Have a look back at Sentence 16, which also uses **might**.

In sentence 27, on the other hand, the use of **will** means that John is deciding at the time of speaking. He is promising to go out (as long as he finishes his work).

APPENDIX FOUR

In sentences 6 and 7, instead of using "If he was ill" and "If your father was here", it is possible to say "If he were ill" and "If your father were here". In fact (strictly speaking) it is grammatically correct to use "were" with the third person singular in **Second Conditional** sentences and incorrect to use "was", but in the real world you will find that many native speakers use "was". Often the student of English knows better than a native speaker when a particular grammar point in English is incorrect. It does lead us to the question of what is right and what is wrong grammatically. The reason I have used "was" in sentences 6 and 7 is that in the real world of colloquial English, in **Second Conditional** sentences, you are just as likely to hear a native speaker saying "was" as you are to hear him/her saying "were". Very often grammar mistakes become so absorbed into mainstream language that they cease to be considered as wrong and become accepted.

APPENDIX FIVE

The intonation used in any sentence is key to understanding the true intention and feeling of the speaker. Here you only have the written sentences. When you hear the sentences on the CD, try and gauge the mood of the speaker and what his/her purpose is.

Take for example sentence 10. It could be spoken in a *frustrated* tone, by a teacher who has little hope that his student is going to start studying more. Or, it could be spoken in a *persuasive* way, giving the impression that there is still time - if the student changes his mind and starts studying more – to salvage the situation and pass the exam. It would be impossible to know the real feeling of the speaker without either the written context (as opposed to an isolated sentence which is all you have here) and/or hearing the sentence spoken and the intonation used.

APPENDIX SIX

Sentence 21 expresses a possibility. The likely context here is that I am deciding on a place to go for a holiday. The decision might be difficult, so I am comparing different advantages - "If I went to Italy I **could** practise my Italian. On the other hand if I went to Brazil, I **could** visit (my friend) Noelia."

Remember that the **Second Conditional** expresses something imaginary. But here we see that the imaginary is something that could easily become real. It is imaginary at the time of speaking because no final decision has been made yet.

In this situation, I am definitely going to take a holiday – Brazil, Italy or somewhere else. Each possibility could easily become reality.

So sentence 21 is expressing a possibility. The sense is that "I *would be able* to visit my friend, and therefore I *probably* would visit them".

The difference between this and sentence 22 is that sentence 22 is a statement of intent – "definitely I will visit...". It is like the use of **will** in the **First Conditional**. It is a decision that the speaker is making, there is a certainty to it. They (the speaker) know that *if* in any future moment they were in Brazil, they would definitely want to visit their friend.

Don't be confused – the certainty of the action (i.e. visiting the friend) depends entirely on whether the speaker goes to Brazil or not. The certainty is not related to the decision of whether to go to Brazil or not, it is related to what the speaker has decided to do if he *does* go.

APPENDIX SEVEN

It's a similar case here. You have decided that you don't like Chinese food even though you have never tried it. You already have a fixed mind about it, and the speaker is trying to encourage you to open your mind, be brave, and the result might be quite different from what you imagine.

In sentence 28 it makes more sense to put something like "I think" to emphasize personal opinion. Why do you think that is the case?

It is because **would** implies something certain, but I can't know for sure that you will like Chinese food if you try it. Maybe you are going to hate it! From the sense of the situation, it would be far more natural to hear native English speakers prefacing the "you would like it" with something that indicated personal opinion – like the "I think" I have put in sentence 28.

This brings us to another point. Why do I think you would like Chinese food?

I am using **would**, which indicates some certainty. Certainty is not based on any guesswork, so the context of this sentence might be something like "I think you would like it, because I know you like other Asian food, and it's probably quite similar."

In other words, the context of sentence 28 must contain some reason as to why I affirm "you would like it." The use of **would** implies that there is something I know, some information that I have, that gives weight to my opinion.

APPENDIX EIGHT

The only difference is in the level of certainty. Remember the **First Conditional** talks about the real world, so if you say, "If I go to Brazil" it means there is an opportunity for you to go, perhaps your friend invited you or there is a possibility to go on a school trip or something.

Using the **Second Conditional** just means that the possibility is more distant, I am only imagining it at the time of speaking. Of course it's possible that in the future I will go to Brazil. But that possibility is not linked to any current circumstances. Using the **Second Conditional** puts you in the imaginary world.

These differences can be quite subtle, but that is the nature of language. Gaining a sense of a language - any language - means developing a feel for, and an understanding of, these nuances of meaning.

APPENDIX NINE

The difference in sentence 30 is more difficult – this is the type of sentence where students are often left feeling confused.

Let's imagine in sentence 30 that a wife is talking to her husband. As a **Second Conditional** sentence, it imagines something that doesn't appear very likely to happen. It is only imaginary at the time of speaking, although at some time in the future it may of course happen. But at the time of speaking, there is little or no evidence to suggest it is going to happen.

The **First Conditional** sentence, on the other hand, is dealing with the real world. So the context of the sentence must be that a discussion has been taking place between the husband and wife about the possibility of the husband moving back home. And the possibility is distinct and real. The wife can sense that her husband is leaning towards the option of moving back.

When you are thinking about whether to use the **First Conditional** or the **Second Conditional** in your speaking or writing, think about whether you are expressing something that belongs to the real world or the imaginary world.

If the possibility is real at the time of speaking, because of the context, use the **First Conditional**. If the possibility is imaginary, use the **Second Conditional**.

APPENDIX TEN

The imaginations of the **Third Conditional** often express *relief* (it's good that things didn't turn out like that!) or *regret* (wishing things hadn't happened the way they did).

Sentences 4, 5 and 6 express *relief*. Sentences 8 and 10 express *regret*. Sentence 2 could be expressing either *relief* or *regret*. From the isolated sentence (i.e. without the context) we can't tell, because we don't know who is talking. An England supporter saying the sentence would be expressing *regret*, but a supporter of the opposing team would probably be expressing *relief*.

APPENDIX ELEVEN

Contractions are more difficult with the **Third Conditional** because they can be used in both parts of the sentence.

Your natural tendency might be not to use them. Native speakers of English however – on both sides of the Atlantic - use them all the time. You will only understand them by developing a familiarity with them. Hearing lots of spoken English as opposed to just reading sentences in a book – will help you to achieve this. And as I have said before, for your personal communication with others to sound as natural as possible, it is vital that you develop your own use of contractions. When you listen and re-listen to the CD, make a point from time to time of focusing only on the use of contractions.

APPENDIX TWELVE

This sentence could be understood in two different ways. Sam could be offering a kind of retrospective advice to Stuart (i.e. "You should have hit him. Why didn't you?").

But maybe Sam is emphasizing a respect he has for Stuart based on the fact that he controlled himself and didn't hit the other person. In effect he could be saying, "I couldn't have controlled my feeling like you did and I would've become violent, which might have made the situation worse."

Without the context and the intonation, we can't know exactly what kind of feeling or intention Sam is expressing.

APPENDIX THIRTEEN

The "If it'd been Dad" carries the implicit sense of "*in that situation*". Let's imagine a context for this one.

Robert's mum wrote a letter of complaint to her bank manager regarding a cheque she wrote that bounced. The bank was at fault. Although the bank corrected the mistake, the letter of complaint was never acknowledged and no apology was offered.

Robert's mum took no further action. Robert knows his father's character, and imagines what he *would have done* in the same situation. He knows his father would have complained much more strongly and would've insisted on an apology and possibly compensation.

Naturally, this kind of sentence depends on the speaker knowing the person he is talking about well enough to be sure of how they would have reacted in the situation.

APPENDIX FOURTEEN

Can you see how using this particular **Mixed Conditional** structure changes the meaning from the use of a pure **Third Conditional**?

Third Conditional sentences, as you know, imagine the opposite action and the opposite result of a past situation. This type of **Mixed Conditional**, instead of focusing on an imaginary past result, focuses on an *imaginary present result*. That is why the conditional tense is used and not the conditional perfect.

In sentence 12, the focus is on the fact of having a *headache now*, at the time of speaking - the present result of last night's action.

In sentence 13, the focus is on the fact that Bernie *is not rich now* (although he could have been).

In sentence 14, the focus is on the fact *you are my wife now - today*, and all because of the fact that we attended the same conference.

These nuances reveal what the speaker is emphasizing to his listener(s). This type of **Mixed Conditional** focuses on a present result of a past action.

APPENDIX FIFTEEN

Do you see how **could** - when expressing a possibility - expresses something in the future?

Compare that to its use when expressing ability. **Could** is the past tense of 'to be able', but in sentences 12, 13, 14 and 16 it is being used to talk about a future possibility. The nature of possibility is concerned with the future - if something has already happened, we know whether it was possible or not.

The only exception to this last point in this group of sentences is the last one - number 20. Can you see why?

The situation is past, therefore the outcome is already known. The sentence expresses an impossibility - how a planned course of action (i.e. going to the concert) turned out to be impossible to carry out because of circumstances beyond our control (i.e. there were no tickets left).

So when **could** is negative, it can be used to express a past impossibility. Otherwise it expresses a *specific future* possibility, i.e. relating to a particular situation.

In the introduction to Part Two, you read that the concepts that **modal verbs** express often overlap. What is meant by this?

Can and **could** both talk about ability and possibility. But sometimes both those concepts are contained within a single use of **can** or **could**.

For example have a look back at sentence 18. The sentence expresses the possibility of the speaker's father being stubborn, in other words, he is so stubborn sometimes. But there is a case for suggesting that the use of **can** equally expresses his ability to be stubborn. The ideas of ability and possibility are not easily separated.

You can see this overlapping of concepts in some of the other sentences as well.

This is not something to worry about. Your level of English – both speaking and writing – does not depend on whether or not you can work out whether a particular use of **can** or **could** is expressing possibility or ability. That can be debatable, like in sentence 18.

Categorizing every single sentence is not necessary for you to develop a sense of English. What you need to be able to do is to feel which **modal verb** to use in a particular context. This takes practice and dedication, and consequently, time.

Your goal is to get to the point where you know instinctively which **modal verb** best expresses what you want to convey. A true 'sense' must be instinctive, as opposed to going through a mental process of categorization.

APPENDIX SIXTEEN

You might therefore assume that the two sentences come from two different situations. That is a wrong assumption to make. They could easily relate to the same situation.

Remember that **modal verbs** don't talk about definite things, they describe people's opinions, moods and feelings. In other words, they reveal individual perspectives. The same situation can be perceived differently by different people.

It is very difficult to explain the nuances of emphasis and intonation in written text! The CD track at the end of this Module will be very helpful for you to develop a feel for what we have been talking about here.

APPENDIX SEVENTEEN

The reality is that language changes and evolves alongside culture, and the main reason that **may** is used less and less is because the culture we live in is itself far less formal than it used to be.

Even in business and professional situations, it is becoming increasingly acceptable to address people more informally. To my native ears, it sounds over-the-top to use **may** now to ask for permission.

So, where might you hear this kind of language? Read sentences 39 and 40 again, and imagine the following context:

The police have to inform John's parents that their son has just been murdered, and then have to ask them some questions about him. It is a situation of extreme sensitivity, and therefore adopting an extremely formal approach is possible and probable.

In terms of everyday language however, you should forget about **may** when you need to ask for permission. You will find that in everyday English native speakers simply don't use it.

APPENDIX EIGHTEEN

When used to ask for a favour or for permission to do something, always remember that **would** indicates a polite attitude.

Many languages use different words to address different people. For example, the word for 'you' might be different depending on whom you are talking to. If you were talking to an older person, a parent or a teacher, you might need to use a polite form of the word 'you' to express the relevant level of courtesy, and it might be rude not to do so.

Old English used to have this sort of distinction, but in the modern language, it is the use of **modal verbs** which can convey politeness or respect.

If I am in the company of somebody important, or indeed just an older person to whom I should show respect, then the use of **would** is appropriate.

APPENDIX NINETEEN

Think about this - without the context to this sentence, we don't actually know if the party has taken place yet or not. The intonation would almost certainly indicate this, but it would take a trained native ear to ascertain just from the words and tone whether the party was in the past or the future.

When you hear sentence 11 on the CD, the intonation will indicate that the party has not taken place yet. The speaker conveys a surprised but pleased tone that their mum will go to the party.

We keep talking about 'a sense of English'. Your goal must be to acquire a sense of the language that enables you to interpret these kinds of subtleties just as a native speaker can. It's far from easy, you need a lot of perseverance and time, but press on.

So the party hasn't taken place yet. The sentence therefore represents (at the time of speaking) an unfulfilled promise. Will my mum go to the party or not? She said she **would**, but when the moment comes, maybe she won't.

The intonation in a sentence like this also enables the listener to determine how much the speaker trusts their mum's statement of intent.

APPENDIX TWENTY

So few students of English seem comfortable with using **might**.

Most students I know – wanting to convey the meaning of sentences 34 and 35 – wouldn't use **might** at all, and would say something like "Maybe I will go to London next year..." or "Maybe

Sean's parents will buy a villa...". Of course, grammatically it is perfectly correct to say this, but native English speakers will usually use **might** in this kind of sentence. It's a classic example of a word that students understand when they hear it, but are not confident to use. That mustn't be your case. To sound natural and fluent in English, you will need to master the use of **might** in your spoken and written language. It is such an important and frequently-used word.

APPENDIX TWENTY ONE

This is a strange one and difficult to explain. Let's give it a context to help us, and imagine that I am the speaker of the sentence and I am talking to you. Curtis is a friend of ours who has recently got divorced.

We have just seen Curtis and you have commented that he seemed to be OK. Then I say the above sentence. It means that I agree with you that he looked OK, but I know that inside he is really not OK and is hurting a lot because of his personal situation. In other words, his outward expression and behaviour is covering up his deep feeling.

The "**might've** looked OK" therefore means that he *only looked* OK (i.e. he wasn't really OK).

This use of **might** precedes a clause in the sentence which tells you that the reality is opposite to what it seemed to be.